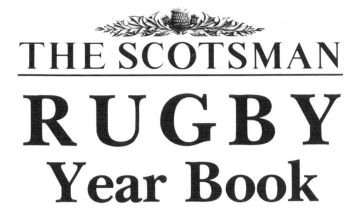

THE SCOTSMAN
RUGBY
Year Book

THE SCOTTISH SEASON
1989-90

NUMBER

1

Harry Pincott

John Davidson

D0264049

SPORTSPRINT PUBLISHING

EDINBURGH

ISBN 0 85976 326 9

Phototypeset by Newtext Composition Ltd., Glasgow.
Printed in Great Britain by Bell & Bain Ltd., Glasgow.

Our thanks to Colorsport for the use of
the colour illustrations used on the cover, and to
Scotsman Publications for the use of the black
and white illustrations accompanying the text.

Contents

The Changing Face of Scottish Rugby

SCOTTISH RUGBY has just finished its 17th season of the National League, currently supported by McEwan's, and while there are many who say the 14-team divisions are still too big there's no doubt the league is here to stay, in one form or another.

The critics are probably right when they say the league's introduction has led to most of the clubs adopting a negative attitude, yet how can you argue against Scotland winning two Grand Slams in the last six years?

And where would clubs like Highland, Stirling County, Portobello, Currie etc be now if they had not had the opportunity to climb up the divisions? Under the system prevailing before the National League came into being it was extremely difficult to break into the unofficial championship. Most clubs' fixtures had a kind of permanent look about them and the aforementioned clubs would have been hard pushed to get games against the likes of Hawick, Gala, West of Scotland etc who were the powers in the land at that time.

However, it was not one of those clubs which won the last unofficial championship, but Boroughmuir, who had previously had to fight hard for recognition even though they had also topped the championship in the early 1950s.

In the 1972-73 season Boroughmuir came out top with a 90 per cent record, followed by Hawick and Gala, both on 85. Jordanhill (82) came next, then Langholm (81) and Edinburgh Wanderers (72), just ahead of Watsonians, Gordonians, West of Scotland and Dunfermline. The bottom four clubs were Aberdeen GSFP, Kelvinside, Edinburgh University and finally Stewart's FP, who were soon to amalgamate with Melville FP.

Other clubs who took part in the championship that year were Trinity Academicals, Perthshire, Leith Academicals, Broughton and Musselburgh, all of whom found life much harder when the National League was formed the following season though they

1

were not alone in that.

Since then Jordanhill, who for many years were one of the country's leading teams – that's when they were coached by Bill Dickinson and had players such as Ian McLauchlan, Richie Dixon, Hugh Campbell, Struan McCallum, John Roxburgh and Gordon Strachan in their line up – have amalgamated with Hillhead while Broughton have slipped down as far as Division V, and have just escaped going lower by the skin of their teeth.

It would surprise a few Goldenacre stalwarts that in the last unofficial championship Heriot's ended up with only 31 per cent with clubs such as Broughton, Hutchesons and Trinity above them.

But while Heriot's staged a revival, thanks to the fact that they had a strong rugby-playing school behind them – and which was soon to give the FP club players such as Andy Irvine, Iain Milne, Peter Steven, Kevin Rafferty etc – other clubs soon found their flow of schoolboys almost drying up completely as teachers and pupils were attracted to other sports.

It did not help them either when more clubs started throwing their doors open to all-and-sundry and competition for players increased. Few people at the start of the 1970s would have envisaged the likes of Heriot's, Edinburgh Academicals, Glasgow High (now Glasgow High-Kelvinside) and Glasgow Academicals going open and the lack of success over the last decade of Stewart's-Melville and Watsonians can be traced to their reluctance to follow suit, though they have slightly relaxed their stance since and it could prove to be their saviour.

Watsonians were as high as seventh in the 1972-73 championship but were relegated two years ago and their first season in that division proved a harrowing experience, even though they had three overseas players in their 1st XV who were led by Scott Hastings.

The days when clubs relegated from Division I jumped straight back into the top division are now long gone as competition for a step up gets hotter and hotter every year. In order to build up their playing resources many clubs have taken on overseas players, though, for instance the success of Currie has been built mostly on local talent who have been blended into a formidable force by coach Graham Hogg.

Currie's achievements have been quite remarkable as it was only ten years ago they were champions of Division VII, following in the footsteps of Stirling County (1976-77) and Portobello (1978-79). Whatever fate holds in store for them in Division I Currie have proved that nothing is impossible if you have foresight and dedication.

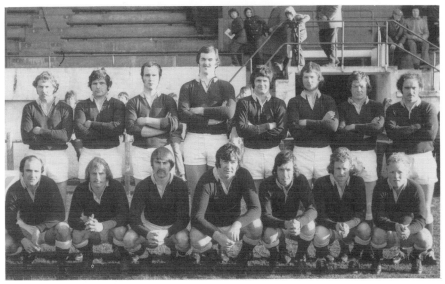

Hawick's championship-winning side of season 1975 76 when they were captained by Ian Barnes (middle front).

Of course when one speaks of dedication the name of Hawick usually springs to mind and while their fortunes have waned over the last couple of seasons few doubt that they will soon be a real force in Division I again. Along with Boroughmuir, Heriot's and West of Scotland (until now), Hawick have the distinction of having been permanent fixtures in Division I, winning the title on no fewer than ten occasions, including the first five in succession.

During that time they set a standard which few teams could match though with players like Jim Renwick (126 league games), Alastair Cranston (121), Norman Pender (59), Colin Deans (144), Colin Telfer (49), Alan Tomes (167 which covers all 17 seasons), Billy Murray, Brian Hegarty (79), Ian Barnes (44), Alister Campbell (121) and more recently Greig Oliver (100), Colin Gass (100), Keith Murray and Derek Turnbull, that was hardly surprising.

Coaching them to many of their successes was former Scotland and British Lions flanker Derrick Grant, a hard taskmaster who was given great assistance by Elliot Broatch. There were times when Hawick looked invincible, their driving forward play and Renwick's genius behind the scrum sweeping all before them. But as they say all good things must come to an end and it did in 1978-79 when Heriot's lifted the title. Twelve years on they are still the only non-Border club to have triumphed.

With Andy Irvine and Iain Milne the catalysts Heriot's produced some glorious rugby, their only setback being a 7-6

David Leslie, key man for Gala in Division I successes and also a magnificent performer for Scotland in their 1984 Grand Slam.

defeat at Netherdale. But that proved to be the only hiccup in a superb season in which the Goldenacre men's record was – played 11, won 10, lost 1, points for 246, against 82.

Heriot's last game was against Haddington and it was just as important to the East Lothian club who had been promoted the previous season. They required both points to stay up but it was not to be. On a bitterly cold day on March 24, 1979 – the Goldenacre pitch had to be cleared of snow to allow the rearranged game to go on – Heriot's won 32-6 with the following XV – Irvine; Bill Gammell, Jim Craig, Harry Burnett, Steve Page; Fraser Dall, Iain Duckworth; Jim Burnett, Callum Munro, Milne, Douglas Lynn, Derek Stephen, Jock Millican, Hamish McDougall and Peter O'Neill.

The coach was John Stent who in his playing days turned out in almost every position behind the scrum and he was assisted by Peter Hill who was responsible for the fitness programme.

Heriot's continued their winning ways at the start of the 1979-80 season, returning from London on the first weekend of September with a magnificent double – the XV-a-side Charrington International Festival Trophy being won at Wembley on the Saturday night and the Harlequins Sevens Cup 24 hours later, a triumph for the following Seven – Gammell, Peter Steven, Irvine, Alan Lawson, David Robertson, Peter Whitelaw and Kevin Rafferty.

However, Heriot's reign at the top of Division I proved to be short lived and it was Gala's turn to be top dogs, though Heriot's did finish runners up only a point behind. The Netherdale club were champions in three seasons – 1979-80, 1980-81, and 1982-83, with Hawick preventing their great rivals from making it four in succession by snatching the title in season 1981-82 when Heriot's were second for the third year on the trot.

These were halcyon days for Gala, who were captained by the redoubtable Jim Aitken for two of their triumphs (David Leslie led in their third title-winning season) and coached by a former Netherdale favourite, Johnny Brown. They formed a formidable partnership, each speaking the same plain language, and while their critics accused them of being very much a ten-man side you can't argue against success, however it is gained. Aitken gathered round him one of the best club packs ever, with such as Ken Lawrie, Bob Cunningham, Tom Smith, Gordon Dickson and Leslie, all internationalists, and such willing grafters as Ken Macaulay and Jock Berthinussen. They had the right scrum-half behind them, David Bryson, the current captain, a man who played to his strengths, and in the middle they used the power of George

Halliday, who rarely failed to make the gain-line.

Add in the accurate boot of full-back Peter Dods and they had a steady point accumulator who could also score and make the odd try or two. Dods, of course, was to make an even greater impact in the 80s as Scotland's Grand Slam full-back.

Gala were also fortunate to have the vastly experienced Arthur Brown, the former Scotland full-back, operating at stand-off and "Hovis" was, like Bryson, much appreciated by his forwards because his trusty left boot kept the ball in front of them. Over their first two championship seasons Gala lost only one league match and were miserly in the number of points conceded, 58 in 1979-80 and only 55 the next season when they won all 11 matches.

Gala's hopes of three in a row were foiled by Hawick in 1981-82, after which the National League was reorganised, with two teams added to each division to bring them up to 14, and a new Division VII was created with the top seven clubs from the West District, four from the East and three from the Midlands.

At stand-off for Hawick was none other than Colin Gass, who had played at centre in Gala's championship-winning team but even Gass's kicking could not stop the title going back to Netherdale in 1982-83 when they won 12 of their 13 games, running up a record points total of 491. In that season Derek White broke through and Jim Maitland took over at stand-off from Brown.

However, once again the pendulum swung Hawick's way and with Renwick, Deans and Tomes now joined by the likes of Gass, Oliver, Turnbull, Paul Hogarth and Sean McGaughey the Mansfield Park club reeled off four championships in a row during which time they lost only three matches, a marvellous record with the highlight being season 1983-84 when they won all 13 games, running up 477 points while conceding only 53.

But Hawick were now being threatened by another Border club, Kelso, who in seasons 1984-85, 85-86 and 86-87 finished runners up, the last-named championship going to Hawick only by way of points differential, both teams finishing on 24 points, with third place going to Watsonians, who were boosted by the Hastings brothers, Scott and Gavin. That was the season Gala, now shorn of most of their caps, were relegated along with Jed-Forest.

However, Kelso, including internationalists Roger Baird, Andrew Ker, Gary Callander, John Jeffrey and Eric Paxton, who were given great support by the likes of Marshall Wright, Ewan Common, Douglas Robeson, Bob Hogarth, Rob Cowe, Alistair Stewart, Clive Miller and Gary Waite, who was forced into

Andy Irvine, whose dashing and exciting play led Heriot's to many thrilling victories.

premature retirement because of a neck injury, had their revenge in 1987-88 when they pipped Hawick for the title, by points differential, after again finishing on 24 points.

Incredibly the following season Kelso, who were playing a most attractive brand of rugby, were for the third time running involved in a points differential finish and this time it was Boroughmuir who lost out, giving the Poynder Park club their second title. Jim Hewit, their coach, was delighted but little did he and his side know what was in store for them in 1989-90.

Kelso, and Hawick as well, found themselves fighting against relegation for much of the season while the newly promoted Gala consolidated their place in the top division and Melrose became the fourth Border club to wear the mantle of Scottish champions.

Melrose could not have timed their burst to the top any better, coming as it did in Keith Robertson's last season, when his final appearance was on tour in Chicago. In their domestic programme Melrose played 30 games of which 28 were won and 812 points were scored (an average of almost 27) while 38 players turned out for the 1st XV with hooker Steven Brotherstone and winger Andy Purves playing in 27 of them and Craig Redpath and Alan Tait in 24.

Though the following XV – Craig Redpath; Andy Purves, Leroux van Niekerk, Graham Shiel, Keith Robertson; Craig Chalmers, Alan Tait; Tom McLeish, Steven Brotherstone, Keith Sudlow, Kenny McLeish, Doddie Weir, Andrew Dobie, Carl Hogg and Andrew Kerr – ended up as the optimum XV, players such as Angus Redburn, Duncan Cameron, Scott Aitken, Robbie Brown and Andrew Redpath all played their parts in what was, without doubt, a team effort coaxed, or should one say demanded, from them by the one and only Jim Telfer, who got as much delight from Melrose's triumph as he did from Scotland's Grand Slam.

With such a young team Melrose look well equipped to defend their title, but one wonders if the National League, after the 1991 World Cup, will continue as it is. Many would like to see eight-team divisions, with home and away fixtures being played, which they say would generate more income. In addition some would also prefer league matches to be played straight off and not broken up as they are now, though where you would accommodate the District Championship, internationals and a Scottish Cup, heaven knows!

However, Scottish rugby, for all its critics, is in a fairly healthy state and is likely to stay that way in the foreseeable future, as long as money, in the shape of professionalism, does not corrupt it. That may be its biggest threat.

Scotland: A Season to Remember

TO ALL EXTENTS AND PURPOSES Scotland's second Grand Slam in only six years was earned with victories over Ireland, France, Wales and England. But there are many within the SRU hierarchy who will tell you that just as important were the wins over Fiji and Romania in October and December respectively and also the experience picked up by those Scots on British Lions tour to Australia, namely Gavin and Scott Hastings, Craig Chalmers, Gary Armstrong, David Sole, Derek White, John Jeffrey, and captain Finlay Calder and coach Ian McGeechan.

They were to do as good a job for their own country as they had done for the Lions with McGeechan going on to be named Coach of the Year.

McGeechan, however, was quick to point out the great job done by his colleague, Jim Telfer, who had guided Scotland to the 1984 Grand Slam, when another prop, Jim Aitken, was captain. This time it was Sole in charge and his influence on events was just as great. A dynamic player in the loose, Sole at last managed to convince the remaining doubters that he was a good scrummager. And just as important, he proved to be an inspiring choice as captain.

While one would have liked to see Scotland play with a lot more flair and panache, it's worth remembering that Armstrong and Chalmers are still relatively inexperienced at international level and the best is yet to come from them.

Tony Stanger will certainly remember his introduction to international rugby, six tries in six games being not a bad return. Derek White, often an unsung hero, had a superb series of games and not far behind were Jeffrey and Calder. Locks Chris Gray and Damian Cronin were a solid and combative boilerhouse, with the mobile Kenny Milne and Paul Burnell making vital contributions to what were a first class pack.

Their camaraderie and will to win pulled them through many tight situations and they were given magnificent support by backs, whose defensive qualities at times bordered on the heroic.

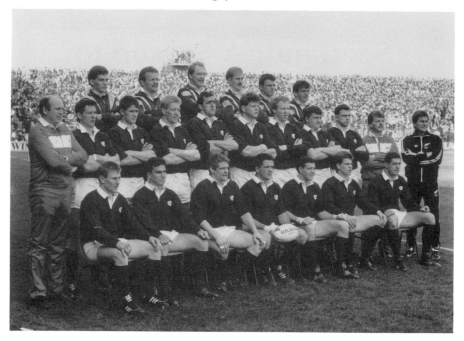

Scotland's Grand Slam squad: Back – Craig Redpath, Alex Brewster, Derek Turnbull, Douglas Wyllie, John Allan, Greig Oliver. Middle – Sean Lineen, Tony Stanger, John Jeffrey, Chris Gray, Damian Cronin, Derek White, Paul Burnell, Kenny Milne. Front – Gary Armstrong, Iwan Tukalo, Finlay Calder, David Sole, Scott Hastings, Craig Chalmers, Gavin Hastings.

Scotland 38, Fiji 17.

On their return from Australia quite a few of the players took a short rest but come the visit of the Fijians to Murrayfield on 28 October only Calder was missing, the Scotland captaincy going to Sole.

The only newcomer to the Scots XV was the 21-year-old Hawick winger, Tony Stanger, a powerfully-built youngster who also had pace and a very effective hand-off. It proved to be a very happy debut for the Borderer who scored two tries and had a big say in Chris Gray's score.

Sole led the forwards with much gusto and there was excellent inter-play between the back-row of Jeffrey, White and Graham Marshall and half-backs Armstrong and Chalmers.

As is their style, the Fijians occasionally produced some glorious handling and running, but Scotland's control up front and the opportunism of Stanger more than offset Fijian flair.

Left: Ian McGeechan has proved himself one of the best coaches in the world.

Right: Jim Telfer's law! Two Grand Slams and a Division I title for Melrose prove just how successful a coach he is.

Scorers – Scotland. *Tries* – Tony Stanger (2), Kenny Milne, Chris Gray, Gavin Hastings and Iwan Tukalo. *Conversions* – Hastings (4).
Penalties – Hastings (2).

Fiji – *Tries* – Lovo, Rasari. *Penalties* – Koroduadua (2), Serevi.

Scotland   C Hastings; A Stanger, S Hastings, S Lineen, I Tukalo; C Chalmers, G Armstrong; D Sole, capt, K Milne, P Burnell, C Gray, D Cronin, J Jeffrey, D White, G Marshall.

Scotland 32, Romania 0.

Scotland's other warm-up game, prior to the Five Nations Championship was against Romania at Murrayfield on 9 December, played half an hour after Scotland and Ireland had drawn 22-22 in a B international. Finlay Calder, fit again, replaced Marshall and Lindsay Renwick, the London Scottish winger, was called in for his first cap in place of the injured Tukalo.

Injury also ruled out Chalmers and the experienced Douglas Wyllie teamed up with Armstrong. Though it was a bigger winning margin than against Fiji, the Scots had to work much harder against a team who seemed to be content to play a containing game.

In fact the home XV led only 9-0 at the interval, but they got on top in the second half and eventually ran out 32-0 winners, with Stanger claiming another three tries and Sole scoring his first try for Scotland.

Heading for a try against Romania is the Scotland No 8 Derek White.

It was after the international that the Romanian lock Christian Raducanu defected and later joined Boroughmuir.

Scorers – Scotland. *Tries* – Stanger (3), Derek White, Sole. *Conversions* – Hastings (3). *Penalties* – Hastings (2).

Scotland – G Hastings; A Stanger, S Hastings, S Lineen, L Renwick; D Wyllie, G Armstrong; D Sole, capt, K Milne, P Burnell, C Gray, D Cronin, J Jeffrey, D White, F Calder.

Ireland 10, Scotland 13.

In the time in between the Romanian match and the first championship fixture, Tukalo and Chalmers had recovered from their ailments and were named in a full strength XV to meet Ireland at Lansdowne Road on 3 February.

A fortnight earlier the Irish had lost to England at Twickenham and so were determined to do well in front of their own crowd.

That determination was evident right from the start and David Sole's men found it hard to get into the game, especially at the lineouts where those two grizzled veterans Donal Lenihan and Willie Anderson were winning more than their fair share of possession.

David Sole on the rampage against Ireland, with Kenny Milne and Damian Cronin in support.

In fact the Irish led 7-0 at the interval through a Michael Kiernan penalty and John Fitzgerald try. But the fighting spirit and team-work, which was to serve Scotland so well in the course of the championship, bubbled to the surface shortly into the second half.

A searing burst by Lineen was supported by Jeffrey who then sent White careering over for a superbly worked try. As Gavin Hastings had missed a few penalty kicks, Sole called on Chalmers to take the conversion and the Melrose stand-off duly obliged.

Kiernan and Chalmers then exchanged penalties, to make it 10-9 for the Irish, but with Scotland proving the fitter and stronger, White picked up from a scrum and sprinted 15 metres for what proved to be the winning score.

Scorers – Ireland. Try – Fitzgerald. *Penalties –* Kiernan (2).
  Scotland – *Tries –* White (2). *Conversions –* Chalmers. *Penalty –* Chalmers.
Scotland – G Hastings; A Stanger, S Hastings, S Lineen, I Tukalo; C Chalmers, G Armstrong; D Sole, capt, K Milne, P Burnell, C Gray, D Cronin, J Jeffrey, D White, F Calder.

Scotland 21, France 0.

On the face of it the visit of the reigning champions should

The powerful Gavin Hastings about to give a French opponent the message!

have been Scotland's hardest game, but in the end, it gave them their biggest winning margin, though that might have been a lot less had the French back-row forward Alain Carminati not been sent off for stamping by referee Fred Howard not long into the second half with the Scots hanging on to a 3-0 lead.

As usual there were squeals from the French but TV showed Carminati going in with the boot and Howard was right. To emphasise the folly of the Frenchman's actions, Chalmers, again replacing Hastings as kicker, landed the resultant penalty and Scotland proceeded to beat France by a record margin.

A long kick by Tukalo had the French defence in a tangle and Lineen hacked on and claimed the try. However, the ball bounced loose again and Calder dived on it. In fact the referee credited Calder with the score, though Lineen still claims it as his.

Tukalo then displayed his pace and strength to the full when he burst through Pierre Hontas's tackle and then took Olivier Roumat over the line with him. Chalmers converted both and added a penalty as the French resistance crumbled.

Scorers – Scotland. *Tries* – Calder, Tukalo. *Penalties* – Chalmers
    (2), Hastings.
Conversions – Chalmers (2).

No wonder the cockerel is frightened for its life as Finlay Calder careers through the French defence.

Scotland – G Hastings; A Stanger, S Hastings, S Lineen, I Tukalo; C Chalmers, G Armstrong; D Sole, capt, K Milne, P Burnell, C Gray, D Cronin, J Jeffrey, D White, F Calder.

Wales 9, Scotland 13.

For the third game running Scotland had to face opposition licking their wounds after defeat by England. Though their club rugby appeared as strong as ever, Wales had difficulty in finding the right blend internationally and new coach Ron Waldron had turned to his own club, Neath, to provide the basis of the XV.

The Welsh, more than any, don't like being beaten at rugby and so it was into the Lions den at Cardiff that Scotland took their unbeaten record. Six years ago they had beaten Wales 15-9 but in the two games in Cardiff since then Wales had come out on top.

It was always going to be hard and physical and that's how the game on 3 March was played. Both sides were restricted to one try each and once again it was the Scots' unquenchable spirit and heroic defensive qualities that saw them through.

Gavin Hastings had another off day with his place kicking, but his handling, fielding and powerful clearing kicks more than made

Bracing himself to fend off a Welsh coverer is Gary Armstrong at Cardiff.

up for those lapses, which might have been crucial had Craig Chalmers not stepped into the breach so well.

The mobility of the Scottish pack was another trump card with John Jeffrey the outstanding forward on the field. At half-time the Scots were more than satisfied to be 10-3 up, two penalties by Chalmers being added to a forward's try, sparked off by Sole and finished by Damian Cronin. Wales's only reward for a lot of pressure was a Paul Thorburn penalty.

The seven-point cushion was soon cut, winger Arthur Emyr crossing for his first international try which Thorburn converted. But the Scots were not to be denied and Chalmers kicked a penalty to make the final score 13-9.

Scorers – Wales. Try – Emyr. *Conversion –* Thorburn. *Penalty –*
   Thorburn.
Scotland – Try – Cronin. *Penalties –* Chalmers (3).
Scotland – G Hastings; A Stanger, S Hastings, S Lineen, I Tukalo;
   C Chalmers, G Armstrong; D Sole, capt, K Milne, P Burnell,
   C Gray, D Cronin, J Jeffrey, D White, F Calder.

Scotland 13, England 7.

With England also having won their three matches, totting up

Build-up to Scotland's try at Cardiff. David Sole is tackled but manages to get the ball inside to the supporting Kenny Milne and Paul Burnell with the touchdown eventually being claimed by Damian Cronin.

83 points in the process to Scotland's almost miserly 47, the encounter at Murrayfield on 17 March was for a glittering array of prizes – the Five Nations Championship, the Calcutta Cup, the Triple Crown, and the coveted Grand Slam.

Princess Anne was there as Patron of the SRU, it was the 50th birthday of the Scotland's forwards' coach, Jim Telfer, and the Flower of Scotland was being given laldy by the Murrayfield crowd who then erupted as the warrior-like David Sole stomped onto the pitch with his team.

The big England pack, according to many sections of the media, were going to teach the Scots a lesson. Sole and his colleagues are still waiting for it. From the whistle the Scots set such a pace that one actually felt sorry for the likes of Paul Rendal, Jeff Probyn and Wade Dooley who were reduced to walking pace late in the game.

As at Cardiff the try count was one each and Scotland's was a

Over goes Damian Cronin for that vital try against Wales.

Two Englishmen can't prevent Gary Armstrong getting the pass away that launched Tony Stanger's try.

New Zealand referee David Bishop signals the most important try of the season, Tony Stanger's effort against England at Murrayfield.

truly memorable effort and fit to grace the occasion. It came almost immediately after the interval with Scotland leading 9-4, thanks to three penalties by Craig Chalmers against a Jeremy Guscott try. From a scrum, Jeffrey fed Armstrong on the blindside and the scrum-half managed to send the supporting Gavin Hastings away. The full-back made ground and then just before he was tackled into touch, he put in a lovely high kick towards the England line.

Storming up in pursuit were Tony Stanger and Finlay Calder and as the ball bounced in the in-goal area it was the Hawick youngster who plucked it out of the air and got the touchdown. It was Stanger's sixth international try in his first season and there's no doubt that he, like Iwan Tukalo, is a deadly finisher.

England then threw all caution to the winds and, after Simon Hodgkinson had cut the deficit to 13-7 with a penalty, Scott Hastings, as only he can, brought off the tackle of the season when he took Rory Underwood from behind as the England winger

John Jeffrey and Gavin Hastings show their true emotions as the whistle goes to end the Scotland-England encounter at Murrayfield.

appeared clean through.

That tackle lifted the Scots' morale and as the English sensed that all their great hopes and ambitions were once again about to be dashed, the Scots finished the game on the attack. When referee David Bishop blew the whistle, the expression on the face of Derek Turnbull, who had come on after 27 minutes of the game in place of Derek White (knee injury) – Turnbull thus became the only change in the four championship games, a remarkable statistic in a remarkable season – said it all. Yes, the Flower of Scotland was in full bloom.

Scorers – Scotland. *Try* – Stanger. *Penalties* – Chalmers (3).
England – *Try* – Guscott. *Penalty* –   Hodgkinson.
Scotland – G Hastings; A Stanger, S Hastings, S Lineen, I Tukalo; C Chalmers, G Armstrong; D Sole, capt, K Milne, P Burnell, C Gray, D Cronin, J Jeffrey, D White (replaced by D Turnbull), F Calder.

Heading through the happy crowd at Murrayfield is Grand Slam captain David Sole. If you want to get ahead, get a hat!

No hiding his delight at Scotland's Grand Slam triumph over England for Bob Munro, convener of the selection committee, seen here with David Sole.

Scotland's Tartan Terrors. All dressed up and ready to begin a night of celebration are David Sole and his Merry Men.

Scotland statistics (six games)

	Tries	Cons	Pens	Pts
C Chalmers	–	3	9	33
G Hastings	1	7	5	33
A Stanger	6	–	–	24
D White	3	–	–	12
I Tukalo	2	–	–	8
D Sole	1	–	–	4
K Milne	1	–	–	4
C Gray	1	–	–	4
D Cronin	1	–	–	4
F Calder	1	–	–	4
Total	*17*	*10*	*14*	*130*

(Five Nations Championship)

	P	W	D	L	F	A	Pts
Scotland	4	4	0	0	60	26	8
England	4	3	0	1	90	26	6
France	4	2	0	2	67	78	4
Ireland	4	1	0	3	36	75	2
Wales	4	0	0	4	42	90	0

Tour Scots Shake the
All Blacks

I SUPPOSE after a team have won the Grand Slam of European rugby the next step is to take on the world champions to find out just how good you are. Well Scotland were fortunate enough to be given that opportunity in May-June and how close they came to providing the greatest ever achievement in Scottish rugby!

The Scots, under the inspiring captaincy of David Sole and coached by Ian McGeechan and Derrick Grant, were unbeaten against the provincial teams but lost both Tests, 31-16 and 21-18.

Before the party left for New Zealand manager Duncan Paterson and other Scottish Rugby Union officials stressed that the tour was very much part of the preparations for the 1991 World Cup and that experience gained, not the results, would be the important factor.

In fact the tour could not have gone much better, even though both Tests were lost. Two new caps were introduced, hooker John Allan (Edinburgh Academicals) being a somewhat controversial choice in place of Kenny Milne (Heriot's) for the first Test – though Milne was recalled for the second international – while the Edinburgh Academicals winger Alex Moore came in for the second Test in place of Iwan Tukalo (Selkirk).

Moore repaid the selectors' faith by scoring an opportunist try from Gavin Hastings' chip ahead and though his enthusiasm caused him to concede a couple of penalties Moore proved on the tour that he has the ability to score tries at the highest level and finished as top tryscorer with four.

While Allan, who has spent much of his life in South Africa since moving there from Glasgow as a youngster, lost his place the hooker more than justified his decision to return to the country of his birth to further his rugby career. Moore and Allan will certainly be important members of the Scotland squad for the World Cup.

After the 31-16 defeat at Carisbrook, where Scotland were well

New Zealand bound. Scotland's tour party board the plane at Edinburgh Airport.

beaten in the lineouts, there were some who thought the selection committee might give the 19-year-old Melrose lock, Dodie Weir, his first taste of international rugby, just as New Zealand had done with the equally young Ian Jones. However, the selectors decided Weir was not quite ready and stayed with Damian Cronin, whose scrummaging power possibly won the day for him.

Having conceded five tries at Carisbrook – the All Blacks scorers being Kieran Crowley, Grant Fox, Ian Jones and John Kirwan (2) with Fox adding four conversions and a penalty – the Scots were determined that they would not make the same mistakes at Eden Park.

In the first Test they had surprised New Zealand by the quality of their back play and Sean Lineen's first try for Scotland, against the country where he was born and raised, was a memorable one. Chris Gray and David Sole also touched down and two conversions by Gavin Hastings brought the Scots total to 16, a lot less than some of their play deserved.

Seven days later Sole's men scored only two points more, but their performance won the hearts and admiration of the crowd at Eden Park and the many millions of TV viewers round the world. They gave as good as they got and even outscored the home XV by two tries to one, a rare occurrence. That they did not win was down to one man, that remarkable kicker, Grant Fox.

The All Black's stand-off had a 100 per cent record with five penalties and the conversion of Richard Loe's try and when you add in his 15 points in the first Test that's a total of 32 out of 52. Fox's style is so simple yet so effective. Gavin Hastings converted the tries by Moore and Tony Stanger, his seventh in only eight internationals, and also banged over two huge first-half penalties. In addition Hastings had a magnificent match in both attack and defence, as did brother Scott.

As in the Five Unions Championship the midfield defence of Scott Hastings, Lineen and Craig Chalmers was superb, Stanger's strength and pace was impressive and Gary Armstrong risked life and limb in his country's cause. No player gave more. Though he was a member of Brewster's Beazers (the midweek XV) Peter Dods was as reliable as ever and finished up as top scorer with 58 points (two tries, 13 conversions and eight penalties). Young Graham Shiel was shaping promisingly until a cut near an eye ruled him out of the later games and there were also excellent contributions from Greig Oliver and Douglas Wyllie.

Up front David Sole continued his super run of form and matching him all the way was the Nottingham lock Chris Gray, who had a first class tour. Gray has, over the past two seasons, blossomed into a world class lock and his support play in the loose was much appreciated by his forwards.

While Finlay Calder stated that the Eden Park Test would be his representative farewell the 28-times capped flanker did also hint that he would be available should his country need him in an emergency. Calder and his back-row colleagues, John Jeffrey and Derek White, were again a dedicated and supportive trio, but there were signs that players like Graham Marshall (3 tries), Adam Buchanan-Smith and Derek Turnbull are not far behind.

Sadly for Turnbull the Hawick flanker suffered a serious groin injury in the game against Manawatu, but the Border policeman will be back. He has proved his resilience before just as Iain Milne has done, the Heriot's prop, who played in both Tests after missing the entire championship.

Milne thus joins the elite band of men who have played international rugby in three decades, the seventies, eighties and nineties. You can't get more resilient than that.

Milne's spirit typifies that of the entire Scotland squad, having rubbed off on the younger uncapped players like Weir, Shiel, Craig Redpath and Buchanan-Smith who must have benefited enormously from the tour, and with the World Cup not being played until the start of the 1991-2 season they will be even better players, which is good news for their clubs as well.

Adam Buchanan-Smith gets ready to dip into a tackle during Scotland's game against Southland at Invercargill on 12 June. The Scots won 45-12.

The experience picked up by all the players should be put to good use at their respective clubs during games, training, etc and the whole of Scottish rugby should reap the benefits of what was a marvellously successful tour.

(Tour party)

Full-backs – P Dods (Gala), G Hastings (London Scottish)
Wings – S Porter (Malone), A Moore (Edinburgh Acads), I. Tukalo
  (Selkirk), A Stanger (Hawick).
Centres – S Hastings (Watsonians), S Lineen (Boroughmuir),
  C Redpath (Melrose), G Shiel (Melrose).
Stand-offs – C Chalmers (Melrose), D Wyllie (Stewart's-Melville).
Scrum-halves – G Armstrong (Jed-Forest), G Oliver (Hawick).
Props – D Sole (Edinburgh Acads), A Brewster (Stewart's-Melville),
  I Milne (Heriot's), P Burnell (London Scottish).
Hookers – K Milne (Heriot's), J Allan (Edinburgh Acads).
Locks – C Gray (Nottingham), D Cronin (Bath), G Weir (Melrose),
  J Richardson (Edinburgh Acads).
Flankers – F Calder (Stewart's-Melville), J Jeffrey (Kelso),
  A Buchanan-Smith (Heriot's), D Turnbull (Hawick).
No 8s – G Marshall (Selkirk), D White (London Scottish).
Officials – *Manager* – D Paterson – *Coaches* – I McGeechan, D Grant.

Scotland tour statistics

MAY 30 – East Coast – Poverty Bay 0, Scotland 45.
SCORERS – *Tries* – G Marshall (2), G Oliver, P Dods, C Chalmers,
  K Milne, S Lineen, D Turnbull. *Conversions* – P Dods (5).
Penalty – Dods.
Scotland – P Dods; A Moore, C Redpath, S Lineen, S Porter;
  C Chalmers, G Oliver; D Sole (replaced by A Brewster), K Milne,
  I Milne, C Gray, G Weir, D Turnbull, G Marshall (replaced by
  D White), F Calder.

JUNE 2 – Wellington 16, Scotland 16.
SCORERS – *Try* – J Allan. *Penalties* – G Hastings (4).
Scotland – G Hastings; A Stanger, S Hastings, G Shiel, I Tukalo;
  D Wyllie, G Armstrong; D Sole, J Allan, P Burnell, J Richardson,
  D Cronin, J Jeffrey (replaced by D Turnbull), D White,
  A Buchanan-Smith.

JUNE 6 – Nelson Bays-Marlborough 6, Scotland 23.
SCORERS – *Tries* – G Marshall, A Moore (2), A Buchanan-Smith,
  Conversions – P Dods (2), *Penalty* – Dods.
Scotland – P Dods; A Moore, C Redpath, G Shiel, S Porter;
  D Wyllie, G Oliver; A Brewster, J Allan, P Burnell, G Weir,
  D Cronin, D Turnbull, G Marshall, A Buchanan-Smith.

JUNE 9 – Canterbury 12, Scotland 21.
SCORERS – *Try* – F Calder, penalty try. *Conversions* –
  G Hastings (2).

Penalties – G Hastings (3).

Scotland – G Hastings; A Stanger, S Hastings, S Lineen, I Tukalo;
C Chalmers, G Armstrong; D Sole, K Milne, I Milne, C Gray,
D Cronin, J Jeffrey, D White, F Calder.

JUNE 12 – Southland 12, Scotland 45.
SCORERS – Tries – S Hastings (2), A Moore, P Dods, G Shiel.
Conversions – Dods (5). *Penalties* – Dods (3). *Drop goals* – D Wyllie
(2).

Scotland – P Dods; A Moore, S Hastings, G Shiel, I Tukalo;
D Wyllie, G Oliver; A Brewster, J Allan, P Burnell,
J Richardson, G Weir, D Turnbull, G Marshall,
A Buchanan-Smith.

JUNE 16 – New Zealand 31, Scotland 16.
*SCORERS – **New Zealand** – Tries* – K Crowley, G Fox, I Jones,
J Kirvan (2).
Conversions – Fox (4). *Penalty* – Fox.
Scotland – *Tries* – S Lineen, C Gray, D. Sole. *Conversions* –
G. Hastings (2).
Scotland – G Hastings; A Stanger, S Hastings, S Lineen, I Tukalo;
C Chalmers, G Armstrong; D Sole, J Allan, I Milne, C Gray,
D Cronin, J Jeffrey, D White, F Calder.
New Zealand – K Crowley; J Kirwan, J Stanley, W Little,
T Wright; G Fox, G Bachop; S McDowell, S Fitzpatrick, R Loe,
I Jones, G Whetton, M Brewer, W Shelford, A Whetton.
Referee – C High (England).

JUNE 19 – Manawatu 4, Scotland 19.
SCORERS – Tries – K Milne, J Richardson. *Conversion* – P Dods.
Penalties – Dods (3).
Scotland – C Redpath; S Porter, P Dods, G Shiel, A Moore,
D Wyllie, G Oliver; A Brewster, K Milne, P Burnell,
J Richardson, G Weir, D Turnbull, G Marshall, A Buchanan-
Smith.

JUNE 23 – New Zealand 21, Scotland 18.
*SCORERS – **New Zealand** – Try* – R Loe. *Conversions* – G Fox.
Penalties – Fox (5).
Scotland – *Tries* – A Moore, A Stanger. *Conversions* – G Hastings
(2). *Penalties* – Hastings (2).
New Zealand – Same as in First Test.
Scotland – G Hastings, A Stanger, S Hastings, S Lineen, A Moore,
C Chalmers, G Armstrong, D Sole, K Milne, I Milne, C Gray,
D Cronin, J Jeffrey, D White, F Calder.
Referee – D Bevan (Wales).

B Men Disappoint

A **22-22 DRAW** with Ireland at Murrayfield on December 9 and an emphatic 31-9 defeat at the hands of France in Oyonnax on January 21 made it a disappointing season for the Scotland B XV.

Against the Irish the Scots made a great start and were 10-0 up in as many minutes, but instead of rubbing in their superiority they sat back and allowed the visitors to match their initiative.

In fact the Irish were 16-10 up at halftime, and though the home men regained the lead at 22-19 with only a minute or two to go they conceded a penalty which stand-off Peter Russell converted.

Included in the Scotland B XV were Stewart Porter, Alex Moore, Dodie Weir and Jeremy Richardson who were later to be selected for Scotland's tour to New Zealand.

A feature of the match was three drop goals by the Scotland B stand-off David Shiel while flanker Derek Busby showed great pace in scoring a fine try.

SCORERS – Tries – A Moore, D Busby. *Conversions –* D Shiel.
Penalty – D Barrett. *Drop goals –* Shiel (3).
Scotland B – D Barrett; A Moore, B Edwards, I Jardine, S Porter, D Shiel, D Bryson, G Graham, K McKenzie, G Wilson, J Richardson, G Weir, J Macklin, capt, D Leckie, D Busby.

About six weeks later a much changed Scotland B XV took on the French at Oyonnax and were soundly beaten by 31-9. The Scots fielded one of their tallest packs, yet once again it was French flair that won the day, though new lock Shade Munro performed well.

Scorers – Penalties – D Barrett (3).
Scotland B – D Barrett; A Moore, P Rouse, B Edwards, S Porter; G Breckenridge, D Bryson; G Graham, I Corcoran, G Wilson, J Richardson, S Munro, A Macklin, capt, A Macdonald, D Busby.

Other Internationals
Under 18s – Netherlands 0, Scotland 32.
Under 19s – Scotland 9, England 17.
Under 21s – Scotland 10, Wales 24.

McEwan's Inter-District Championship

Glasgow not miles better, but . . .

THOUGH they had claimed a share of the McEwan's Inter-District Championship three times between 1975-78, it was back in season 1973-74 that Glasgow had last won the title outright.

Therefore their success this season was all the more gratifying for rugby in the west of Scotland especially as they had finished second bottom the previous year, a solitary victory over North and Midlands being their only success.

However the new coaching partnership of Richie Dixon, who should really be awarded a DSM for his services to Glasgow rugby, and former Watsonians and Scotland centre, David Johnston, had instilled a new sense of pride and determination in the squad, and the captain, Fergus Wallace (Glasgow High-Kelvinside), was to prove an excellent leader.

Two games in Ireland at the beginning of September, a 21-6 win against Connacht in Galway and an 18-18 draw against Munster in Limerick, got their season off to a spirited start, the results being not so important as the team spirit fostered during the weekend.

As well as being part of the warm-up for the inter district championship these two games got the players into the right frame of mind for their glamour game of the season, against the touring Fijians at Hughenden on October 25.

The Fijians had only the two games in Scotland and both ended in defeat, Glasgow's victory being followed by a national triumph three days later at Murrayfield.

Glasgow's display against the tourists was an eye-opener to their supporters. Their forwards, and in particular their Stirling County front-row of George Graham, Kevin McKenzie and Brian Robertson, got stuck into their bigger opponents and the backs responded with some great attacking rugby, sparked off in many cases by their new stand-off George Breckenridge (Glasgow High-Kelvinside).

31

Against Fiji Glasgow scored four tries, through Alan Watt, Derek Stark, Kevin McKenzie and Ian Jardine, with David Barrett converting three of them for a 22-11 victory.

While obviously delighted the two Glasgow coaches were at pains to stress that "one swallow does not make a summer" and that the first district game, against champions Edinburgh on November 25, would show just how much progress the side had made.

Well, Glasgow proved they were catching up fast by drawing 19-19 and, in fact, were denied their first inter-city victory since 1983 only by a last gasp penalty by Peter Steven (Heriot's FP).

Both teams deserve credit for their display considering the game was moved from an unplayable Hughenden to New Anniesland shortly before the scheduled kick-off, and in the end the only disgruntled people were the TV crew who could not move their equipment to the new venue in time.

Glasgow's new found belief in themselves took them into 16-9 and 19-13 leads but inexperience at times let their rivals off the hook. And in the end the home side were fortunate to get a draw as Edinburgh raised their game considerably in the last quarter and if the game had lasted another five minutes they would have won.

SCORERS – **Glasgow** – *Tries* – G Breckenridge, K McKenzie, *Conversion* – D Barrett. *Penalties* – Barrett (3).
Edinburgh – *Tries* – F Calder (2). *Conversion* – P Steven. *Penalties* – Steven (3).

Glasgow – D Barrett; M Duncan, D McKee (all West of Scotland), I Jardine (Stirling County), D Stark (Ayr); G Breckenridge, E McCorkindale (both Glagow H-K); G Graham, K McKenzie, B Robertson, S Hamilton (all Stirling County), A Watt; D Busby, F Wallace (all Glasgow H-K), D McVey (Ayr).

Edinburgh – S Douglas (Boroughmuir); P Steven, D Stoddart, (both Heriot's), S Lineen, M Debusk (both Boroughmuir); D Wyllie (Stewart's-Melville), J Dun (Edinburgh Acads); A Brewster (Stewart's-Melville), K Milne (Heriot's), G Wilson, J Price (both Boroughmuir), J Richardson (Edinburgh Acads), K Rafferty (Heriot's), S Reid (Boroughmuir), F Calder (Stewart's-Melville).

Glasgow's next encounter was a fortnight later against the North and Midlands and once again the men from the west were involved in a change of venue. The original venue, Inverness, was under snow and so was Murrayfield. Eventually after many phone calls

More like football than rugby as David Leckie (North and Midlands) and South's Roger Baird let fly at a ball at Netherdale.

Hawkhill, Leith Academicals' pitch in Edinburgh, was found to be playable, though in the event the bitter wind and driving rain almost proved too much for the players, officials and spectators.

However, the players did remarkably well scoring five tries, Glasgow claiming three of them in a 19-10 victory in which the Hillhead-Jordanhill lock, David Jackson, made a notable debut.

SCORERS – **North and Midlands** – B Bell, M Allingham. *Conversion* – C Macartney.

Glasgow – *Tries* – P Manning, D Stark, D Barrett. *Conversions* – Barrett (2). *Penalty* – Barrett.

North and Midlands – H Murray (Heriot's); C Macartney, B Edwards (both Boroughmuir), P Rouse (Dundee HSFP), D McLaughlin (Boroughmuir); C Evans (Aberdeen GSFP), M Allingham (Heriot's); G Mackenzie (Highland), M Scott (Dunfermline), J Scobbie (Stirling County), B Bell (Highland), I Paxton (Selkirk), H Edwards (Boroughmuir), D Leckie (Edinburgh Acads), B Ireland (Stirling County).

Glasgow – D Barrett (West); D Stark (Ayr), D McKee (West), I Jardine (Stirling), P Manning (Ayr), G Breckenbridge, E McCorkindale (both Glasgow H-K); G Graham, K McKenzie,

B Robertson (all Stirling County), A Watt (Glasgow H-K),
D Jackson (Hillhead-Jordanhill), D Busby, F Wallace (both
Glasgow H-K), D McVey (Ayr).

With three points from their two games Glasgow were now
championship contenders and to stay in that position they had to
beat the South at the Greenyards on December 23. A tall order
indeed, even though the South were not going well, having beaten
North, but losing 16-15 to the Anglo-Scots.

It was not to be a spectacular match, but the greater
commitment of the Glasgow pack won them the game. The
Borderers, especially behind the scrum, made too many handling
errors and the no-cap Glasgow XV well deserved their 22-10
victory over a home side who fielded six caps.

Once again Breckenridge, given excellent service from
McCorkindale, kicked soundly and big Alan Watt had a storming
game in the loose.

SCORERS – **South** – *Try* – R Baird. *Penalties* – P Dods (2).
Glasgow – *Tries* – A Watt, D Stark, P Manning. *Conversions* –
    D Barrett (2). *Penalties* – Barrett (2).

South – P Dods (Gala); A Stanger (Hawick), H Hogg, A Douglas
    (both Jed-Forest), R Baird (Kelso); D Shiel, G Armstrong;
    N McIlroy (all Jed-Forest); I Corcoran (Gala), K Sudlow
    (Melrose), S Graham (Hawick), G Weir (Melrose), G Marshall
    (Selkirk), C Hogg (Melrose), J Jeffrey (Kelso).
Glasgow – D Barrett (West); D Stark (Ayr), D McKee (West),
    I Jardine (Stirling County), P Manning (Ayr); G Breckenridge,
    E McCorkindale (both Glasgow H-K); G Graham, K McKenzie,
    B Robertson (all Stirling County), A Watt (Glasgow H-K),
    D Jackson (Hillhead-Jordanhill), D Busby, F Wallace (both
    Glasgow H-K), D McVey (Ayr).

With the Anglo-Scots, coached by David Leslie and Alan Friell, also
having won their three games, the scene was all set for a district
decider between them and Glasgow at Burnbrae on December 30.

A huge crowd turned up to watch the home side triumph by
18-15 to win the championship. Glasgow's hero was full-back David
Barrett who landed six penalties, outkicking his more illustrious
opposite number Gavin Hastings, who after missing a few kicks,
was replaced by Nick Grecian.

Barrett's winning kick came in the last minute and was
absolutely crucial because if it had remained at 15-15 the Anglos
would have taken the title for the first time. But Glasgow were not
to be denied and though Richie Dixon admitted his mainly young
XV had surprised him by finishing as champions – "I thought it

Jock Dun, Edinburgh's scrum-half, does not know it, but just after getting the ball away he is about to be flattened by a flying Brian Ireland (North and Midlands) at Goldenacre.

was a season too early to expect the big breakthrough" – there was no happier man in Scottish rugby that night.

It was not a free-flowing exhilarating game of rugby, but physical and tense. The Anglos lost international lock Damian Cronin (back injury) at half-time, Logan Mair being the replacement. Though he played well the loss of Cronin, especially in the lineouts, was crucial to the outcome of the game.

For the Anglos Richard Cramb dropped two goals and Grecian converted his own try as well as landing a penalty.

*SCORERS – **Glasgow** – Penalties – D Barrett (6).*
Anglos – *Try – N Grecian. Conversion – Grecian. Penalty – Grecian. Drop goals – R Cramb (2).*

Glasgow – D Barrett (West); D Stark (Ayr), I Jardine (Stirling County), D McKee (West), P Manning (Ayr); G Breckenridge, E McCorkindale (both Glasgow H-K); G Graham, K McKenzie, B Robertson (all Stirling County), A Watt (Glasgow H-K), D Jackson (Hillhead-Jordanhill), D McVey (Ayr), F Wallace, D Busby (both Glasgow H-K).

Anglo-Scots – G Hastings; N Grecian (both London Scottish),
A Warwood (Leicester), D Caskie (Gloucester), L Renwick;
R Cramb (both London Scottish), S Jardine (S Glamorgan) Inst);
D Butcher, B Gilchrist, P Burnell (all London Scottish), C Gray
(Nottingham), D Cronin (Bath), J Macklin, D White,
A Buchanan-Smith (all London Scottish).

At the same time as Glasgow were beating the Anglos, Edinburgh were putting on what was, arguably, the best performance in the championship, a 40-12 drubbing of the South at Myreside.

With their forwards in command the capital backs took some time to get going, but in the last quarter two inspired moves by Sean Lineen paved the way for superb tries by fellow centre Scott Hastings.

Overall, however, it was a disappointing championship for Edinburgh, who had won the title the three previous seasons. They failed to play to their potential, especially against the North and Midlands and the Anglos.

Once again the North finished with no points, yet they still contrived to play some glorious rugby, especially against Edinburgh. One of their tries, scored by Derek McLaughlin, stemmed from a move started on their own line and their adventurous approach deserved better reward.

However, the Dundee HSFP centre, Paul Rouse, won a B cap, alongside North colleague Brian Edwards, and it won't be long before North win a district game.

The Anglos certainly made an impact with hard-fought wins over Edinburgh, South and North and with the likes of Gavin Hastings, Lindsay Renwick, Stewart Jardine, Paul Burnell, Chris Gray, Damian Cronin, Jeremy Macklin and Derek White around the title could be theirs in the very near future.

McEwan's District Championship

November 25	–	Glasgow 19, Edinburgh 19;
		South 23, North and Midlands 6
December 2	–	Anglo-Scots 16, South 15;
		Edinburgh 25, North and Midlands 22
December 16	–	Anglo-Scots 12, Edinburgh 9;
		North and Midlands, 10, Glasgow 19.
December 23	–	North and Midlands 9, Anglo-Scots 15;
		South 10, Glasgow 22.
December 30	–	Glasgow 18, Anglo-Scots 15;
		Edinburgh 40, South 12.

An open-mouthed Mike Allingham (North and Midlands) watches opposite number Ewan McCorkindale get a pass away in the game against Glasgow at Hawkhill. On left is referee Ray Megson.

(How they finished)

	P	W	D	L	F	A	*pts*
Glasgow	4	3	1	0	78	54	7
Anglo-Scots............	4	3	0	1	58	51	6
Edinburgh	4	2	1	1	93	65	5
South	4	1	0	3	60	84	2
North-Midlands.....	4	0	0	4	47	82	0

While the South had their poorest district championship for many years their Under 21s, led by the Melrose No 8, Carl Hogg, won the Scottish Under-21 title, by a point from Glasgow.

Coached by the Hawick duo of Colin Deans and Robbie Welsh, the South youngsters ran in 21 tries and conceded only four. Top try scorers were Gala's Michael Dods and the Jed-Forest pair, Barry Hughes and Callum Brown with three each. Dods also added 28 points with his boot.

Scottish Under-21 Championship

	P	W	D	L	F	A	*pts*
South	4	3	1	0	119	47	7
Glasgow	4	3	0	1	66	64	6
Edinburgh	4	2	0	2	54	64	4
Anglo-Scots............	4	1	1	2	44	59	3
North-Midlands.....	4	0	0	4	38	97	0

Boroughmuir prop Grant Wilson takes on an opponent in Scotland's B International against Ireland at Murrayfield with Dodie Weir coming up in support.

McEwan's National League

DIVISION 1

Melrose join elite band

BY WINNING the Division 1 title in the McEwan's National League for the first time, Melrose became only the fifth club to have achieved that feat, joining Hawick, champions on no fewer than ten occasions, Gala three, Kelso two and Heriot's one. Melrose also won the Border League, which they did by new year, a record for the competition.

And the Greenyards club could not have timed their success any better, coming as it did in Keith Robertson's last season and shortly after their coach, Jim Telfer, had played a major part in Scotland's Grand Slam triumph.

Melrose eventually won the division by a point from Heriot's and Jed-Forest, but they did have a game in hand against Stewart's-Melville which was never played. The champions lost only one game in what was probably the surprise result of the season in Division 1, Ayr winning 9-8 at the Greenyards. But even that inspirational victory was not enough to save the Millbrae men from relegation, along with West of Scotland.

However, like the champions they proved to be, Melrose put that result behind them and in their very next game they scored what they saw as one of their crucial wins, a triumph over Boroughmuir at Meggetland where the young Melrose lock, Robbie Brown, typified the Melrose spirit by playing for almost all the match with a bad knee injury.

Brown was one of the mainly young Melrose XV to emerge with flying colours this season and four of them, Craig Chalmers, Craig Redpath, Graham Shiel and Dodie Weir, were selected for Scotland's tour of New Zealand.

Chalmers, of course, was the key man in the Melrose side, contributing 136 of his side's 247 points, one of his vital kicks being a long-range penalty winner against Heriot's at Goldenacre. Chalmers' appetite for the game is enormous and considering he is only 21 Melrose can look forward to many more years' service from him.

Melrose, winners of Division I and Border League.

Chalmers finished top scorer with 208 points in just 17 appearances while Leroux Van Niekerk and Andy Purves led the tryscorers with 11 each. Melrose won 33 of their 35 games, the last five being achieved on a successful tour of Chicago, where Robertson played his last game for his beloved club.

The arrival of South African centre Leroux Van Niekerk was also significant for Melrose as it gave them a physical presence in midfield and when Robertson, the captain, who missed the first few months of the season because of a knee injury sustained in South Africa during the summer, returned he mostly played on the left wing.

Another three players who figured prominently were teenage hooker, Stephen Brotherstone, who took over from B cap, George Runciman, now retired, and the big No 8, Carl Hogg, while the gritty and durable Alan Tait had arguably his best season for the club.

While Melrose's style was based on hard, driving forward play they did answer their critics at times by playing some spectacular rugby, witness the games against Stirling County, Boroughmuir and Jed-Forest.

With such a young side – half of them are 22 or under – Melrose should be able to look forward to a very successful nineties, during which time they and Jed-Forest look as if they may become the dominant Border clubs, taking over from Kelso and Hawick.

There was a time in the season when the former champions were both in danger of relegation, but to their credit they came away and in Tony Stanger and John Jeffrey Hawick and Kelso

Crunch time for the Melrose scrum-half Alan Tait as he is tackled by Stuart Reid at Meggetland.

respectively had two of the season's personalities.

Of the other clubs Heriot's did well to finish second, a points differential, in their Centenary season, but that success was tempered by the retirements, at the early age of 30, by district stalwarts Peter Steven and Kevin Rafferty. They also won the River Series Trophy.

Jed-Forest, inspired by Gary Armstrong, continued their improvement, as did Edinburgh Academicals who, however, like Boroughmuir, flattered to deceive at times, especially the Meggetland men, even with Romanian Christian Raducanu in their ranks.

But outside of Melrose, most kudos must go to Stirling County who, in their first season in Division I, confounded many people by finishing fifth, after taking the scalps of Stewart's-Melville, Hawick, Kelso, Heriot's and Boroughmuir in front of their enthusiastic supporters at Bridgehaugh. Stirling's achievements were quite remarkable and in George Graham, Kevin McKenzie and Brian Robertson they had an outstanding front row.

In possession is the young Melrose No 8, Carl Hogg, in the match against Heriot's at Goldenacre.

Mike Allingham on the break for Heriot's against Melrose at Goldenacre where the Borderers won with a late penalty by Craig Chalmers.

Heriot's Centenary flag ready to be run up by an all-international cast of (left to right) Peter Steven, Kenny Milne, Andy Irvine and Iain Milne.

Iain Milne, the Heriot's captain, gets an upside-down look at life during the game against Hawick.

DIVISION II

Wanderers back at last

It was in season 1976/77 that Edinburgh Wanderers last played in Division I, but after a lengthy time in the wilderness the Murrayfield club, after several near misses, won Division II and promotion after a highly successful season.

Coaches Bill Hamilton and David Tweedie had hoped to go up with an unbeaten record, but they came a cropper against Currie at Malleny Park, their only blemish on an otherwise spotless season in which they scored 332 points in their 13 league games.

Right from the start Hamilton and Tweedie, after a meeting with players, put the emphasis on 15-man attacking rugby and their refreshing attitude was amply rewarded, their burly, but speedy winger, Graeme Stirling ending up with ten league tries, the best record in Divisions I and II. He was Scotland's top tryscorer with 27.

Dan Pulfrey, the former Scottish Schools full-back, was also a very important player for the club, scoring 113 league points and, for example, in a crucial game against Preston Lodge, displaying excellent handling and kicking skills in wet and windy conditions. Pulfrey ended the season with 250 points, including 14 tries.

In the past team spirit has sometimes been lacking in Wanderers sides, but that was not the case this time with Hamilton's three sons, captain Grant and Keith and Les, playing in the back division alongside the younger Craig brothers, Bryan and Murray. Bryan, the stand-off, had an excellent season and he and Murray have the ability to make an impact on Division I.

As for Tweedle it was an emotional season for him because when he went on as a replacement against Kilmarnock it meant the centre-cum-winger had played for the Wanderers over four decades, his first game being way back in the 1960s. And, of course, it was so rewarding for Bill Hamilton, who was in his second spell at Wanderers, and had suffered so many frustrating setbacks.

With a new clubhouse being built at the end of Murrayfield Ice Rink – Greenside Lodge having been sold – Wanderers, one of Scotland's first open clubs, are set fair for a new spell of prosperity, on and off the field.

But as far as the field is concerned they will have to do it without Fife farmer Robin Orr, an inspirational figure in the Wanderers, but who at the age of 37, and after two broken legs, will not play again, though he will help out on the coaching side.

Wanderers' only conquerors, Currie, finished runners-up and so will step up to Division I for the first time, an amazing feat for a club who just over ten years ago were still playing in the Edinburgh District League.

"A team without any stars", was how coach Graham Hogg described his side who relied on experience in the shape of captain John Cockburn, top scorer Ally Donaldson (109 pts) and Pete Farrer, plus outstanding youngsters in prop David Wilson and winger Scott Forrester, eight league tries.

Currie's success, which should be a shining example to others, has been achieved by hard work and commitment, and these qualities will be needed as they size up their next venture – a stand.

Watsonians, even with Scott Hastings and an influx of New Zealanders and Australians, had a very disappointing season and never looked like bounding straight back and were actually in danger of relegation. In fact, they called up two 40-year-old forwards, Jimmy Stewart and Mark Watters, to see them through, the two sides relegated being Dalziel and Gordonians.

DIVISION III

Dundee HSFP

Points, points, glorious points . . . would have been an appropriate chorus for Mayfield supporters who saw their side emerge with the best record in the McEwan's National League.

In the 13 games Dundee ran up a staggering 446 points, while conceding only 100, and were the only team not to lose a match.

Their haul of 25 points was the highest and for that they had mainly to thank teenage stand-off Jon Newton who weighed in with 162 points (4 tries, 43 conversions and 20 penalties) while top tryscorer was Scotland B centre Paul Rouse with 15, followed by David Tully and Paul Shirazi with ten each.

Dundee also kept the momentum going in friendlies and their overall record read – played 26, won 22, lost 3, drew 1, points for 782, against 201. Newton's haul of 261 was a club record and Tully ended up with 22 tries, two more than Shirazi.

While David Leslie, the 1986 Grand Slam flanker, has been a leading light in the club's efforts over the past two seasons to get into Division II he was only one of a coaching committee which, according to president David Nicol, raised the playing standards throughout the three teams.

Coaching co-ordinator was former player Gordon Burnett and under him were Sandy Hutcheson, Ron Smith, Dr Tom Dymock, and Derek and Jimmy Lawson. As Nicol said, "There was no use of having players with talent if we did not have the coaches to bring out that talent."

The emergence of the burly Rouse was a highlight for the club, the centre playing well enough in the District Championship to earn his first B cap. However, Rouse would be the first to admit that at club level he was greatly helped by New Zealander Paul Bernay who played inside centre.

Another New Zealander Dean Newman formed a formidable back-row with Guthrie Batchelor and Alistair Keys while other notable contributions were made by scrum-half and captain Gordon Low and their 40-year-old lock David Melville who missed only one game – a tribute to his fitness and enthusiasm.

While the 1st XV swept almost all before them it was the same for the 2nd XV who won their Midlands League, and the 3rd XV who lost only two matches. The club well deserved their Team of the Month award in January while 13 of them were in the Dundee Select, organised by Leslie, who went to France and inflicted a defeat on Orléans.

There was also joy for Royal High who clinched the other promotion spot. The club have led a rather nomadic existence since quitting Jock's Lodge almost three years ago. However, thanks to the efforts of captain Alan Wardrop, Andy Middlemiss, Graham Duff, Ronnie Collard, Dave Armstrong, to mention but a few, Royal High have survived and are now based in a spanking new £750,000 clubhouse at Barnton.

From such a sound base the club, who also owe a great debt to president Hugh MacKenzie, who has occupied that post for the last nine years, should go from strength to strength.

But while it was delight for Dundee HSFP and Royal High, it was misery for Morgan Academy FP who were relegated along with East Kilbride, whose points differential was minus 55 compared to Haddington's minus 52.

DIVISION IV

Perthshire

In spite of losing two of their first five league games, including the very first at Dumfries, Perthshire then maintained a 100 per cent record in the remainder of their matches to win the championship.

They finished three points ahead of Peebles, who thus clinched promotion after being denied by points differential in a three-way tie the previous season.

The reason given for Perthshire's transformation was the acquisition of a new coach in Allan Quinn who, of course, had worked before with the likes of Boroughmuir, West of Scotland, Heriot's and Scottish Universities.

Quinn immediately re-organised the coaching side with help from No 8 John Beedie and former prop Chris McGuiness and with only two new faces in the 1st XV, full-back Rod McCrae and teenage lock David Barnett, who played for Scottish Schools the previous season, Perthshire became a very well-drilled XV.

McCrae, previously with Edinburgh Academicals, and Dunfermline, emerged as a key man, sharing the kicking duties with stand-off Sid House. Centre Mike Birch was top tryscorer and there were sterling contributions from captain Gavin Drummond and his younger fellow-prop, Jim White, centre Ken Mackay, a former captain, and scrum-half Ian Halliday, the ex-Edinburgh Wanderers flanker.

Praise is also due to two players who were used as replacements, centre Lorne Bayne, and prop Sandy Hay, whose father Chuck was one of Scotland's top curlers.

Mind you, it was not only Perthshire's 1st XV who had a good season. Their blooming youth section, embracing minis, midis, colts and Under-18s, went from strength to strength, those helping out including convener Jock Halley, James Dalgleish, Brian Simpson, Bob Petrie and Bob Lindsay.

In fact, Simpson organised a tournament for primary schools in the area and on the first Saturday over 150 boys, who previously never had any contact with a rugby club, turned up. It's something other clubs may want to try, as Perthshire see it as an investment for the future.

Just as the season ended Perthshire had to move out of their clubhouse at North which has been taken over by Perth and Kinross Council, who will refurbish and lease it back to the rugby club.

The two clubs relegated were Alloa and Paisley, the latter after just one season in the division.

DIVISION V

Lismore

To say that Lismore won the championship and promotion by the skin of their teeth would have been the understatement of the season. They actually achieved it with the very last kick of their very last game on March 10.

The venue was Memorial Fields, home of Ardrossan who themselves needed the two points to go up. And they looked like doing that when leading 9-7 with literally seconds to go. But Ardrossan conceded a penalty and up stepped Steve Thomson to strike it between the posts and Lismore were champions, by points

Lismore, winners of Division V.

differential from Waysiders.

It was appropriate that Thomson scored the winning points because the winger, who plays cricket for Heriot's, and full-back Jamie Milne are the only survivors from the team who gained promotion to Division V back in 1983.

Since then Thomson has regularly been top tryscorer and leading points gatherer for the Edinburgh club who play in Inch Public Park. In the league games, Thomson scored 14 tries, eight penalties and eight conversions with Milne contributing eight tries, four conversions and three penalties. For the season Thomson must have scored between 250-300 points, about his average.

Captained by back-row forward Chris Campbell, Lismore were fortunate enough to obtain the services of Alasdair Cuthbertson as coach, the man who masterminded Portobello's climb up the national league.

Cuthbertson managed to get the best out of the players, including newcomers Andy Saunders (ex Madras) and centre-cum-wing Graham Mitchell, formerly of Strathendrick. With big Alan Soden (32) the key figure in a hefty pack Cuthbertson made sure that Lismore used the ball wisely, making full use of the narrow side.

These tactics paid off handsomely and complemented the strong team spirit which pervaded the club who, at times, turned out five teams, another notable achievement for a club with no feeder. In fact Lismore called on only 20 players during their league campaign and you can't get better than that.

There was another notable achievement when the club won their own sevens tournament for the first time with the following side – Thomson, Milne, John Glen, Kenny Inglis, Alastair Barclay, Douglas Anderson and Soden. They also were triumphant in the Holy Cross sevens and over-35s event.

But while it was a great season for Lismore poor Lenzie were relegated for the second year running along with Aberdeen University.

DIVISION VI

North Berwick

Winning a sevens tournament would hardly be most people's idea of a turnabout in a club's 1st XV fortunes, but as far as North Berwick are concerned that's exactly what happened.

In April 1989, after a very disappointing season in which they had to beat Walkerburn in the last league game to stay up, which they achieved, North Berwick then confounded even their most ardent supporters by winning their own sevens cup.

That was followed by the choice, which proved inspirational, of winger Derek Grierson as captain, and such was his determination, enthusiasm and dedication that the 1st XV swept through their Division VI programme, winning all 12 games until they came to the final hurdle.

But with the championship already won North Berwick fell to Stewartry and the two points gained were enough to clinch promotion for the Castle Douglas club. If Stewartry had lost St Andrews University would have gone up, on points differential.

While Grierson was undoubtedly the catalyst behind North Berwick's success he would be the first to admit he had great support from his triumvirate of player-coaches, Peter Gillies, Paul Hawker and Bruce Cockburn, who all played in the 1st XV, though injuries restricted Cockburn's appearances to the first half of the season.

Another influential figure proved to be Clive Martin, who got together a bigger selection committee who worked closely with Grierson and the coaches.

With committee and players all pulling their weight the 1st XV went on to win 20 of their 27 games in which they scored 399 points and conceded 241. The 2nd XV were not quite up to that standard, winning only 11 of their 25 matches. North Berwick also managed to put out a 3rd XV on nine occasions.

Leading points gatherer was Edinburgh District Union full-back Graham Elder who totalled 157 points (including 14 tries) while Grierson emerged as top tryscorer with 16. Elder's efforts earned him the club's Player of the Year Award.

While there was plenty of experience in the side in the shape

North Berwick, winners of Division VI.

of Gillies, "about 40", Grierson, Cockburn etc, two youngsters who made the breakthrough were back-row forwards Gary Cunningham and Keith Wilson.

With Hawker a teacher at the school, who won the Scottish Schools cup a few years ago, there is a close link, though during the teachers' strike North Berwick showed their determination to make rugby available to youngsters by starting a midi section, run by Clive Martin and Ian Cunningham.

The midis have now been augmented by a minis section and both are doing well. The club well deserved their McEwan's Club of the Month Award in February.

Not so fortunate were Old Aloysians and Panmure who were relegated.

DIVISION VII

Lasswade clean up

Without doubt it was Lasswade's most successful season ever. Winners of Division VII, by a point from Falkirk and Forrester, they went on to lift the Murrayfield Cup for the first time by beating Duns in the final at Meggetland, brought back the Highland sevens trophy and were runners up in the Penicuik Shield and the Holy Cross sevens.

And all that was achieved by the same players who had won only six of their 13 league games the previous season. But the difference was that they made fewer mistakes and though they scored only 200 points, the lowest total of any of the divisional champions, Lasswade conceded only 93.

Lasswade, winners of Division VII.

The experience gained in the previous seasons stood them well and after beating Forrester in their second League game they knew they were in with a chance. Lasswade's only defeat was at the hands of Falkirk and the two points gained were enough to win Falkirk promotion, by points differential from a frustrated Forrester.

Top tryscorer for Lasswade was their bulky, but cheerful winger, Sandy Roy, with 18, about his average for the past 14 seasons, while the kicking duties were shared by scrum-half Alan Wallace, who did not play after January because of injury, and stand-off Tom McGaw.

Once again the club were coached by the former Haddington player, George Wood, with prop Billy Knowles following in father Bob's footsteps by captaining them. Among his more senior players were Andy Evans, 39, Ally Bain and Stevie Dick, while the youngest, and most promising player, was full-back Steve Smith.

There's always one hard luck story in every club and at Lasswade it revolved around Graham Wright, older brother of Boroughmuir's B prop, Peter, who learned his rugby at Lasswade. Graham was a regular in the second row, but on returning from the Welsh international weekend he was struck down by appendicitis. He lost over five stones in weight and the next time Graham plays rugby it could well be as a 12 stones wing forward, and not a 16 stones lock!

But while it was joy for Lasswade and Falkirk it was despair for Strathmore, Stobswell FP and Dalkeith, who lost their places in the National League. They were replaced by RAF Kinloss, Whitecraigs and Holy Cross, who won a replayed game with Ferranti, the original being abandoned by the referee because of an unruly crowd.

The Sevens

Randwick take sevens honours

IN THE SEVEN major Border seven-a-side tournaments there were five winners, with Jed-Forest achieving a double at Hawick and Langholm, the Saltires winning at Gala, Randwick at Melrose, Kelso at Jed-Forest while at the start of the season Selkirk triumphed at their own tournament and a week later Kelso did the same at Poynder Park.

However, though Jed-Forest and Kelso had two wins each, the highlight of the abbreviated game's season was Randwick's victory on 14 April at a very wet and cold Greenyards.

It was the Australian club's first visit to Melrose and whether it was coincidence or not a record crowd of almost 15,000 turned up to watch the men from Down Under win the Bell's Islander 100th Melrose sevens, beating Kelso 26-8 in the final.

Any seven that have David Campese in their lineup, not to mention Mark Ella, must start favourites and right from the start the Australians showed an appreciation of sevens, having three big forwards who could give their speedy backs plenty of possession. It also helped that the visitors had been resident in Melrose for almost a week and had prepared conscientiously for the tournament.

While Randwick were capturing the crowd's hearts with their brand of play there was just as much support for two other teams. Not surprisingly Melrose were one and Kelso the other, both for similar reasons. Making their final appearances in the Melrose sevens in the colours they had graced for over 15 years were Keith Robertson and Andrew Ker, two superb sevens players.

Nothing could have made Melrose's retiring captain happier than a winner's medal at his own tournament, but sadly it was not to be. And it was that man Campese who shattered Robertson's dreams. In a pulsating semi-final, Melrose were actually leading 15-12 with only seconds to go when Campese virtually slid almost five metres for the winning try.

In the other semi-final, Kelso, the holders, inspired by Ker, playing his last season with the Poynder Park side, made short work of Hawick who went down 22-4. Thus Kelso had reached the

Melrose final for the 11th time in the last 13 years and Ker and Eric Paxton had played in them all.

But as Ker admitted afterwards, Kelso were "never in the hunt," Randwick making light of the conditions to win 26-8, with the Australians' tries coming from replacement centre John Flett (2), Campese, Gavin Boneham and Michael Cheika. Paxton and Clive Millar scored tries for the game losers.

Not surprisingly, Campese emerged as top scorer with seven tries and eight conversions for a total of 44 points and the Australian winger will be welcome to return any time he wants.

Semi-finals – Hawick 4, Kelso 22; Randwick 16, Melrose 15.
Final – Kelso 8, Randwick 26.

Kelso – D Robeson, S Wichary, A Ker, P Dunkley, E Paxton, C Millar, J Jeffrey.
Randwick – D Campese, J Flett, A Niuqila (replaced by D Phillips), M Ella, G Boneham, J Maxwell, M Cheika.

Three in row for Saltires

The previous week at Netherdale the Saltires lifted the Gala trophy for the third year running, the remaining survivors from the previous year being Simon Hunter (Rosslyn Park) and Chris Mantell, Hunter being the only non-Harlequins player in the seven, who defeated Gala 26-14. The guest side had far too much pace in the shape of Everton Davis and John Eagle, not to mention the power of stand-off Simon Hunter, and only in the final were they threatened, having seen off Melrose 24-4 in the semi-final.

In the other semi-final Gala were making their supporters extremely happy by disposing of London Scottish 24-10, their third big victory of the afternoon after 30-4 and 34-4 triumphs against Langholm and Edinburgh Academicals respectively, Mark Moncrieff claiming nine tries in these three ties.

In the final, Saltires' tries came from Craig Luxton (2), Eagle (2) and Peter Winterbottom while Gala replied through Michael Dods, Jim Maitland and John Amos.

Semi-finals – London Scottish 10, Gala 24; Saltires 24, Melrose 4.
Final – Gala 14, Saltires 26.

Gala – M Moncrieff, B Learmonth, J Maitland (replaced by J Turnbull), M Dods, N Crooks, R McCrirrick, J Amos.
Saltires – E Davis, J Eagle (both Harlequins), S Hunter (Rosslyn Park), C Luxton, P Winterbottom, C Mantell, P Brady (all Harlequins).

Melrose Sevens. David Campese scores a last-minute try for Randwick against Melrose in the Final.

Armstrong inspires Jed-Forest

On 21 April at Mansfield Park Jed-Forest retained the Hawick silverware, thanks to the fearless Gary Armstrong who teamed up well with new stand-off Kevin Amos. Jed were almost beaten in the first round by Langholm and their overall success was due to a never-say-die spirit. They had to show that in their semi-final when Harry Hogg scored the winner in the sixth minute of extra time to pip Hawick. Jed's opponents in the final, Selkirk, were also having to work hard for their successes and in the first round it was only a late Scott Nichol try that took them past Melrose.

In the final Jed were again behind after an early Paul Minto try but gradually the Riverside Park men fought their way back. At 18-16 in their favour in the second-half it was anybody's game, but then Amos snatched the winner, converted by Gregor McKechnie. Jed's other tries came from Hogg, Amos and Ronnie Kirkpatrick. Nichol and Keith Johnston got Selkirk's other tries.

Semi-finals – Hawick 12, Jed-Forest 16 (after extra time); Selkirk 20, Glasgow H-K 12.
Final – Jed-Forest 24, Selkirk 16.

56

Jed-Forest – H Hogg, G McKechnie, K Amos, G Armstrong,
R Kirkpatrick, K Liddle, N McIlroy.
Selkirk – D Hunter, K Johnston, S Nichol, T Knox, I Paxton,
P Minto, G Marshall.

Penalty winner by Ker

At Riverside Park a week later, there was the almost unique sight of a sevens tournament being won by a penalty kick. It was kicked by Andrew Ker in injury time and gave Kelso a 19-18 victory in the final over Hawick. It took Ker's total for the afternoon to 37 points and gained him his 96th sevens medal.

For the second successive week four Border clubs reached the semi-finals with the big crowd quietened by the departure of their favourites, going down to a spirited Hawick side. In the second semi Kelso dismissed Melrose.

It was a spirited final. Hawick actually led 12-4 at half-time and 18-16 with the referee looking at his watch. A penalty was then awarded to Kelso and Ker banged it over to give his side an unexpected success. Most of the seven had been at their dinner the previous evening, though like all good players, they had taken it easy.

Semi-finals – Hawick 14, Jed-Forest 6; Melrose 12, Kelso 22.
Final – Hawick 18, Kelso 19.
Hawick – N Bannerman, A Stanger, G Oliver, D Patterson,
S McGaughcy, J Hay, D Willison.
Kelso – D Robeson, S Wichary, A Ker, P Dunkley, C Millar,
A Roxburgh, E Paxton.

Jed-Forest create record

Having won the Langholm sevens for the previous four years, it was a very determined Jed-Forest side who set off for Milntown. And their joy was unconfined when they raced through the tournament to make it five in a row and then completed a marvellous weekend by winning the Halifax sevens 24 hours later.

It was a much-changed Jed side who eventually beat the surprise packets, Aspatria, in the final, with Brian Hughes, Calum Brown and Barry Hughes all being called up and Gregor McKechnie being switched to scrum-half.

Kevin Amos again showed his liking for sevens by running in ten tries, while Harry Hogg, who has appeared in all five Langholm victories, presented his medal to a Riverside stalwart, Bill Purdie.

Hawick Sevens. Scott Nichol scores the winning try against Melrose in the Final.

In the final, Jed-Forest went 20-0, but Aspatria who had beaten Boroughmuir in the semi-final – the only capital club to have reached that stage in the spring circuit – hit back to make it 24-14. However, Jed were not to be denied and ran out 30-14 winners. Their try scorers were Amos (2), Hogg (2), Brian Hughes and Neil McIlroy. Ian Barclay, Paul McGee and Mark Southward scored for the Cumbrians.

Semi-finals – Jed-Forest 24, Hawick 14; Aspatria 18, Boroughmuir 12.
Final – Jed-Forest 30, Aspatria 12.

Jed-Forest – H Hogg, Brian Hughes, K Amos, G McKechnie, Barry Hughes, C Brown, N McIlroy.
Aspatria – M Southward, I Barclay, P McGee, G Doggart, N Wedgewood, T Borthwick, A Grant.

Pow voted top player

Selkirk kicked off the 1989-90 season by winning their own tournament at Philiphaugh and also having their scrum-half Rodney Pow voted Player of the Tournament, just pipping his colleague, Keith Johnston, for the award.

Pow collected four tries and ten conversions and Johnson six tries, one less than Melrose winger Andy Purves. Selkirk's triumph was due to their superior fitness and pace, Scotland winger Iwan Tukalo running in four tries and forwards Iain Paxton and Graham Marshall showing up well in the loose.

Their opponents in the final were Melrose, who scored the only try in their semi-final against Gala, but it was enough to win. However, Selkirk imposed their authority on Melrose right from the start and were 18-0 up, through tries by Pow (2) and Tukalo. Purves scored a late consolation try for his side.

Semi-finals – Jed-Forest 12, Selkirk 20; Gala 0, Melrose 4.
Final – Selkirk 18, Melrose 6.

Selkirk – I Tukalo, K Johnston, S Nichol, R Pow, I Paxton,
I Jeffrey, G Marshall.
Melrose – A Purves, A Redburn, C Chalmers, B Redpath, C Hogg,
A Redpath, C Redpath.

Kelso once again

A week later at Poynder Park there was no stopping Kelso as they romped to their sixth triumph in the last nine seasons, the home crowd being in good voice as their favourites beat Saltires 20-4 in the final. Not for the first time Andrew Ker was top scorer with 40 points and he, Paxton and Bob Hogarth have appeared in all six winning sevens. Full-back Marshall Wright was a strong-running centre and well deserved his six tries.

With Edinburgh Borderers, London Scottish, Saltires and the Welsh Dragons involved there was plenty of good competition for the Border clubs, but none had Kelso's team-work and sevens knowledge. Though Saltires opened the scoring in the final through Richard Moon, the home club then got into their stride and tries followed by Bob Hogarth and Wright who got two each, with Ker landing two conversions.

Semi-finals – Jed-Forest 16, Kelso 24; Saltires 28, Welsh Dragons 6.
Final – Kelso 20, Saltires 4.
Kelso – D Robeson, M Wright, A Ker, R Hogarth, E Paxton,
G Callander, J Jeffrey.
Saltires – K Wyles, S Hunter (both Rosslyn Park), J Thomson (Kirkcaldy), R Moon (Harlequins), D Tosh, A Cushing (both London Scottish), T Coker (Oxford Univ).

59

No sevens round up would be complete without a mention of the Cathay Pacific Hong Kong tournament, now the biggest in the world. Representing Scotland were the Scottish Border Club, who included Harry Hogg, Roger Baird, Tony Stanger, Craig Chalmers, Gary Armstrong, John Jeffrey, Eric Paxton, Ronnie Kirkpatrick and Ian Corcoran.

The Borderers lost 20-12 to New Zealand in the quarter-finals, Hogg getting both tries. In their previous ties the SBC had beaten Sri Lanka 24-0 and Japan 30-0 but the All Blacks' overall pace was their trump card. They went on to beat Barbarians 24-6 in the semi-finals, and then met Fiji, who had cuffed Wales 34-6, in the final.

For once the All Blacks met players who were just as strong and fast as them and the South Sea islanders upset the holders to win 22-10. With nearly all countries being represented by their national teams, one wonders how long it will be before Scotland follow suit.

And at the end of a very long, long season, at the beginning of June in fact, the Saltires won the Lisbon International tournament, beating holders Cambridge Past and Present 32-20.

Whitewash for the Schools

SIX GAMES, six defeats spelt an unhappy season for the Scottish Schools and their coach Rob Moffat. With quite a change in personnel from the previous season it was hardly surprising that the new-look side took so long to settle with one of their best results being in the last fixture, against Ireland.

However, there were some good individual performances from full-back Murray Thomson (Stewart's-Melville), who played in all six matches, centre Kenneth Milligan (Stewart's-Melville), captain on all six occasions, left wing Mark Craig (St Aloysius) who won five caps, half-backs Scott Gilliland (North Berwick) and Gregor Townsend (Galashiels Academy) and forwards Tom Smith (Rannoch), Mark Rutherford (Merchiston Castle), Jim McKechnie (Dundee HS), Murray Rudkin (Watson's) and Richard Lockhart (Heriot's).

The Under-15s had only one game and they went down 0-22 to Wales at Dundee.

In the Bank of Scotland Scottish Schools Cup final at Murrayfield St Aloysius gained revenge on holders Galashiels Academy by beating them 19-15 in an exciting final.

Scottish Schools 8, France 15

M Thomson (Stewart's-Melville); J Anderson (Merchiston Castle), P Crawford (Morrison's Acad), K Milligan (capt. Stewart's-Melville), M Craig (St Aloysius); G Townsend (Galashiels Acad), S Gilliland (North Berwick HS); R Hastings (Kelvinside Acad), M Rutherford (Merchiston Castle), A Mason (Glasgow Acad), D Hathway, M Rudkin (both George Watson's Coll), R Lockhart (George Heriot's), B Millar (Berwickshire HS), M McNeil (Ross HS). Replacement – A Gray (Galashiels Acad) for R Lockhart.

Wales 15, Scottish Schools 0

M Thomson (Stewart's-Melville); J Anderson (Merchiston Castle), K Milligan (capt. Stewart's-Melville), R Erikkson (Merchiston Castle), M Craig (St Aloysius); G Townsend (Galashiels Acad), S Gilliland (North Berwick HS); R Hastings (Kelvinside Acad),

c

M Rutherford (Merchiston Castle), J McKechnie (Dundee HS),
D Hathway, M Rudkin (both George Watson's Coll), M McNeil
(Ross HS), B Millar (Berwickshire HS), R Lockhart (George
Heriot's).

Scottish Schools 7, Scottish Youth 27

M Thomson (Stewart's-Melville); S Tait (Kelso HS), K Milligan
(capt. Stewart's-Melville), R Erikkson (Merchiston Castle),
M Craig (St Aloysius); G Townsend (Galashiels Acad), S Gilliland
(North Berwick HS); R Hastings (Kelvinside Acad),
M Rutherford (Merchiston Castle), J McKechnie (Dundee HS),
D Hathway, M Rudkin (both George Watson's Coll), R Lockhart
(George Heriot's), J Forest (Kelvinside Acad), T Smith
(Rannoch).

Scottish Schools 19, Japan 31

M Thomson (Stewart's-Melville); J Anderson (Merchiston Castle),
K Milligan (capt. Stewart's-Melville), R Erikkson (Merchiston
Castle), M Craig (St Aloysius); G Townsend (Galashiels Acad),
S Gilliland (North Berwick HS); T Smith (Rannoch),
M Rutherford (Merchiston Castle), J McKechnie (Dundee HS),
D Hathway, M Rudkin (both George Watson's Coll), M Browne
Stranraer Acad), R Lockhart (George Heriot's), M McNeil (Ross
HS). Replacements – S Tait (Kelso HS) for M Craig; P Darroch
(St Aloysius) for D Hathway; A Mason (Glasgow Acad) for
J McKechnie.

Scottish Schools 6, England 32

M Thomson (Stewart's-Melville); J Anderson (Merchiston Castle),
K Milligan (capt. Stewart's-Melville), R Erikkson (Merchiston
Castle), M Craig (St Aloysius); G Townsend (Galashiels Acad),
S Gilliland (North Berwick HS); T Smith (Rannoch),
M Rutherford (Merchiston Castle), J McKechnie (Dundee HS),
M McNeil (Ross HS), M Rudkin (George Watson's Coll),
M Browne (Stranraer HS), P Darroch (St Aloysius), R Lockhart
(George Heriot's). Replacements – S Tait (Kelso HS) for
M Craig; G Thomson (George Watson's) for M Thomson.

Ireland 14, Scottish Schools 10

M Thomson (Stewart's-Melville); J Anderson (Merchiston Castle),
K Milligan (capt. Stewart's-Melville), R Erikkson (Merchiston
Castle), N Penny (Stewart's-Melville); G Towsend (Galashiels

Murray Thomson, the Stewart's-Melville and Scottish Schools full-back, in full flight for Lothian Schools against Glasgow Schools.

Acad), S Gilliland (North Berwick HS); R Hastings (Kelvinside Acad), M Rutherford (Merchiston Castle), J McKechnie (Dundee HS), D Hathway, M Rudkin (both George Watson's Coll), M Browne (Stranraer Acad), M McNeil (Ross HS), R Lockhart (George Heriot's).

McEwan's National League 1989/90 Results

September 23

DIVISION I

Selkirk	19	Gala	21
Stirling County	18	Stew/Melv FP	9
Hawick	7	Melrose	18
Jed-Forest	19	Ayr	4
Heriot's FP	25	Edinburgh Acads	7
Boroughmuir	40	West of Scotland	0
Glasgow High/Kelv	13	Kelso	10

DIVISION II

Watsonians	20	Glasgow Acads	9
Hillhead/Jord	13	Langholm	6
Dalziel HS FP	22	Dunfermline	10
Corstorphine	19	Edinburgh Wands	21
Kirkcaldy	9	Currie	9
Musselburgh	15	Kilmarnock	15
Gordonians	15	Preston Lodge FP	26

DIVISION III

Royal High	36	Morgan Acad FP	3
Grangemouth	24	Howe of Fife	19
East Kilbride	12	Wigtownshire	17
Highland	6	Portobello FP	16
Aberdeen GS FP	7	Haddington	19
Dundee HS FP	45	Biggar	0
Clarkston	15	Trinity Acads	14

DIVISION IV

Alloa	6	St Boswells	13
Dumfries	17	Perthshire	14
Penicuik	20	Cambuslang	3
Paisley	3	Cartha QP	13
Leith Acads	4	Peebles	23
Linlithgow	13	Greenock Wands	9
Hutchesons'	30	Edinburgh Univ	14

DIVISION V

Aberdeenshire	3	Dunbar	26
Aberdeen Univ	20	Livingston	31
Lenzie	6	Murrayfield	10

64

DIVISION V continued

Hillfoots	10	Lismore	14
Madras College FP	11	Waysiders	24
Moray	10	Ardrossan Acads	19

DIVISION VI

St Andrews Univ	36	Drumpellier	3
Cumbernauld	29	Earlston	6
Marr	7	Clydebank	16
Walkerburn	9	North Berwick	18
Harris Acad FP	18	Panmure	10
Montrose	12	Stewartry	12
Carnoustie HS FP	23	Old Aloysians	12

DIVISION VII

Rosyth & District	12	Falkirk	9
Strathmore	19	Lasswade	15
Duns	37	Birkmyre	9
Ross High	14	Garnock	17
Cumnock	19	Forrester FP	23
Irvine	60	Stobswell	0
Dalkeith	7	Garioch	10

September 30

DIVISION I

Melrose	33	Selkirk	9
Gala	17	Stirling County	9
Hawick	12	Jed-Forest	19
Stew/Melv FP	6	Edinburgh Acads	34
Ayr	3	Boroughmuir	38
West of Scotland	10	Glasgow High/Kelv	19
Kelso	18	Heriot's FP	29

DIVISION II

Dunfermline	12	Watsonians	13
Glasgow Acads	34	Hillhead/Jord	16
Dalziel HS FP	15	Corstorphine	21
Langholm	40	Currie	13
Edinburgh Wands	16	Musselburgh	4
Kilmarnock	40	Gordonians	3
Preston Lodge FP	19	Kirkcaldy	9

DIVISION III

Wigtownshire	20	Royal High	11
Morgan Acad FP	3	Grangemouth	22
East Kilbride	25	Highland	6
Howe of Fife	33	Haddington	6
Portobello FP	10	Dundee HS FP	28
Biggar	3	Clarkston	4
Trinity Acads	18	Aberdeen GS FP	20

DIVISION IV

Cambuslang	16	Alloa	3
St Boswells	24	Dumfries	3
Penicuik	15	Paisley	9
Perthshire	30	Peebles	17
Cartha QP	14	Linlithgow	12
Greenock Wands	13	Hutchesons'	13
Edinburgh Univ	0	Leith Acads	6

DIVISION V

Murrayfield	29	Aberdeenshire	0
Dunbar	51	Aberdeen Univ	6
Lenzie	6	Hillfoots	38
Livingston	10	Waysiders	14
Lismore	31	Moray	13
Broughton FP	19	Madras College FP	20

DIVISION VI

Clydebank	19	St Andrews Univ	11
Drumpellier	0	Cumbernauld	13
Marr	18	Walkerburn	6
Earlston	25	Panmure	10
North Berwick	15	Montrose	3
Stewartry	23	Carnoustie HS FP	19
Old Aloysians	16	Harris Acad FP	21

DIVISION VII

Birkmyre	10	Rosyth & District	18
Falkirk	52	Strathmore	6
Duns	26	Ross High	12
Lasswade	11	Forrester FP	6
Garnock	6	Irvine	12
Stobswell	15	Dalkeith	4
Garioch	16	Cumnock	6

October 7

DIVISION I

Gala	3	Melrose	27
Jed-Forest	22	Stew/Melv FP	18
Stirling County	16	Hawick	15
Selkirk	16	Boroughmuir	9
Edinburgh Acads	16	Kelso	3
Heriot's FP	41	West of Scotland	0
Glasgow High/Kelv	25	Ayr	6

DIVISION II

Glasgow Acads	60	Dunfermline	6
Corstorphine	30	Langholm	16
Hillhead/Jord	7	Dalziel HS FP	6
Watsonians	3	Musselburgh	3
Currie	19	Preston Lodge FP	11
Kirkcaldy	6	Kilmarnock	14
Gordonians	15	Edinburgh Wands	33

66

DIVISION III

Morgan Acad FP	6	Wigtownshire	15
Highland	9	Howe of Fife	3
Grangemouth	19	East Kilbride	3
Royal High	12	Dundee HS FP	12
Haddington	6	Trinity Acads	11
Aberdeen GS FP	14	Biggar	21
Clarkston	10	Portobello FP	3

DIVISION IV

St Boswells	11	Cambuslang	0
Paisley	12	Perthshire	29
Dumfries	21	Penicuik	3
Alloa	7	Linlithgow	16
Peebles	40	Edinburgh Univ	3
Leith Acads	6	Greenock Wands	30
Hutchesons'	12	Cartha QP	13

DIVISION V

Dunbar	6	Murrayfield	7
Hillfoots	21	Livingston	6
Aberdeen Univ	13	Lenzie	7
Aberdeenshire	42	Moray	6
Waysiders	24	Broughton FP	10
Madras College FP	13	Ardrossan Acads	7
Glenrothes	13	Lismore	25

DIVISION VI

Drumpellier	6	Clydebank	3
Walkerburn	13	Earlston	12
Cumbernauld	23	Marr	15
St Andrews Univ	22	Montrose	0
Panmure	9	Old Aloysians	7
Harris Acad FP	3	Stewartry	12
Carnoustie HS FP	7	North Berwick	9

DIVISION VII

Falkirk	44	Birkmyre	0
Ross High	6	Lasswade	6
Strathmore	10	Duns	15
Rosyth & District	16	Irvine	12
Forrester FP	23	Garioch	10
Cumnock	31	Stobswell	7
Dalkeith	3	Garnock	22

October 14

DIVISION I

Stew/Melv FP	9	Heriot's FP	22
Ayr	29	Gala	22
Boroughmuir	16	Jed-Forest	7
Selkirk	3	Glasgow High/Kelv	19
Melrose	29	West of Scotland	10
Stirling County	29	Kelso	10
Hawick	9	Edinburgh Acads	16

DIVISION II

Langholm	19	Kirkcaldy	13
Edinburgh Wands	16	Glasgow Acads	7
Musselburgh	22	Corstorphine	6
Watsonians	22	Gordonians	25
Dunfermline	9	Kilmarnock	6
Hillhead/Jord	13	Preston Lodge FP	12
Dalziel HS FP	20	Currie	24

DIVISION III

Howe of Fife	10	Aberdeen GS FP	12
Portobello FP	11	Morgan Acad FP	6
Dundee HS FP	56	Highland	3
Royal High	39	Clarkston	14
Wigtownshire	10	Biggar	6
Grangemouth	25	Trinity Acads	10
East Kilbride	24	Haddington	9

DIVISION IV

Perthshire	29	Leith Acads	6
Cartha QP	16	St Boswells	12
Linlithgow	9	Paisley	19
Alloa	24	Hutchesons'	10
Cambuslang	9	Greenock Wands	8
Dumfries	22	Edinburgh Univ	3
Penicuik	0	Peebles	20

DIVISION V

Livingston	3	Madras College FP	10
Lismore	10	Dunbar	14
Moray	6	Hillfoots	18
Aberdeenshire	15	Glenrothes	3
Murrayfield	3	Ardrossan Acads	19
Aberdeen Univ	6	Broughton FP	16
Lenzie	12	Waysiders	24

DIVISION VI

Earston	21	Harris Acad FP	6
North Berwick	13	Drumpellier	7
Montrose	12	Walkerburn	6
St Andrews Univ	16	Carnoustie HS FP	12
Clydebank	9	Stewartry	12
Cumbernauld	16	Old Aloysians	12
Marr	19	Panmure	4

DIVISION VII

Lasswade	34	Cumnock	4
Garnock	3	Falkirk	50
Irvine	13	Ross High	7
Rosyth & District	27	Dalkeith	14
Birkmyre	20	Stobswell	16
Strathmore	9	Garioch	21
Duns	3	Forrester FP	9

October 21

DIVISION I

Ayr	10	Stew/Melv FP	13
Boroughmuir	31	Gala	9
Glasgow High/Kelv	9	Jed-Forest	15
West of Scotland	18	Selkirk	28
Kelso	9	Melrose	9
Edinburgh Acads	22	Stirling County	15
Heriot's FP	23	Hawick	0

DIVISION II

Edinburgh Wands	31	Langholm	10
Musselburgh	18	Glasgow Acads	23
Gordonians	15	Corstorphine	12
Kilmarnock	27	Watsonians	17
Preston Lodge FP	15	Dunfermline	9
Currie	22	Hillhead/Jord	0
Kirkcaldy	50	Dalziel HS FP	9

DIVISION III

Portobello FP	22	Howe of Fife	16
Dundee HS FP	41	Morgan Acad FP	3
Clarkston	10	Highland	6
Biggar	18	Royal High	13
Trinity Acads	24	Wigtownshire	18
Haddington	0	Grangemouth	12
Aberdeen GS FP	19	East Kilbride	18

DIVISION IV

Cartha QP	8	Perthshire	6
Linlithgow	12	St Boswells	9
Hutchesons'	20	Paisley	0
Greenock Wands	9	Alloa	3
Edinburgh Univ	9	Cambuslang	15
Peebles	42	Dumfries	3
Leith Acads	27	Penicuik	0

DIVISION V

Lismore	32	Livingston	3
Moray	12	Dunbar	8
Glenrothes	10	Hillfoots	6
Ardrossan Acads	19	Aberdeenshire	3
Broughton FP	6	Murrayfield	24
Waysiders	32	Aberdeen Univ	6
Madras College FP	18	Lenzie	4

DIVISION VI

North Berwick	10	Earlston	6
Montrose	6	Drumpellier	13
Carnoustie HS FP	27	Walkerburn	13
Stewartry	13	St Andrews Univ	18
Old Aloysians	0	Clydebank	36
Panmure	15	Cumbernauld	22
Harris Acad FP	14	Marr	7

DIVISION VII

Garnock	12	Lasswade	18
Irvine	10	Falkirk	17
Dalkeith	10	Ross High	22
Stobswell	4	Rosyth & District	16
Garioch	13	Birkmyre	11
Forrester FP	39	Strathmore	0
Cumnock	7	Duns	13

November 4

DIVISION I

Stew/Melv FP	15	Boroughmuir	9
Gala	26	Glasgow High/Kelv	3
Jed-Forest	24	West of Scotland	4
Selkirk	28	Kelso	33
Melrose	15	Edinburgh Acads	9
Stirling County	18	Heriot's FP	13
Hawick	28	Ayr	3

DIVISION II

Langholm	16	Musselburgh	3
Glasgow Acads	22	Gordonians	9
Corstorphine	12	Kilmarnock	12
Watsonians	9	Preston Lodge FP	19
Dunfermline	9	Currie	29
Hillhead/Jord	16	Kirkcaldy	3
Dalziel HS FP	3	Edinburgh Wands	32

DIVISION III

Howe of Fife	14	Dundee HS FP	15
Morgan Acad FP	31	Clarkston	12
Highland	0	Biggar	16
Royal High	19	Trinity Acads	6
Wigtownshire	18	Haddington	17
Grangemouth	9	Aberdeen GS FP	15
East Kilbride	4	Portobello FP	14

DIVISION IV

Perthshire	16	Linlithgow	3
St Boswells	12	Hutchesons'	32
Paisley	6	Greenock Wands	12
Alloa	11	Edinburgh Univ	15
Cambuslang	9	Peebles	6
Dumfries	26	Leith Acads	6
Penicuik	4	Cartha QP	8

DIVISION V

Livingston	6	Moray	0
Dunbar	16	Glenrothes	17
Hillfoots	17	Ardrossan Acads	4
Aberdeenshire	15	Broughton FP	9
Murrayfield	9	Waysiders	11
Aberdeen Univ	8	Madras College FP	25
Lenzie	0	Lismore	11

DIVISION VI

Earlston	23	Montrose	0
Drumpellier	18	Carnoustie HS FP	3
Walkerburn	15	Stewartry	17
St Andrews Univ	59	Old Aloysians	3
Clydebank	24	Panmure	6
Cumbernauld	27	Harris Acad FP	0
Marr	0	North Berwick	10

DIVISION VII

Lasswade	19	Irvine	10
Falkirk	49	Dalkeith	3
Ross High	45	Stobswell	0
Rosyth & District	18	Garioch	10
Birkmyre	0	Forrester FP	26
Strathmore	3	Cumnock	18
Duns	8	Garnock	0

November 11

DIVISION I

Glasgow High/Kelv	18	Stew/Melv FP	0
West of Scotland	15	Gala	16
Kelso	9	Jed-Forest	23
Edinburgh Acads	20	Selkirk	18
Heriot's FP	22	Melrose	24
Ayr	15	Stirling County	18
Boroughmuir	23	Hawick	10

DIVISION II

Gordonians	9	Langholm	16
Kilmarnock	12	Glasgow Acads	9
Preston Lodge FP	26	Corstorphine	6
Currie	22	Watsonians	16
Kirkcaldy	7	Dunfermline	6
Edinburgh Wands	47	Hillhead/Jord	20
Musselburgh	24	Dalziel HS FP	9

DIVISION III

Clarkston	19	Howe of Fife	12
Biggar	15	Morgan Acad FP	9
Trinity Acads	20	Highland	3
Haddington	11	Royal High	12
Aberdeen GS FP	3	Wigtownshire	26
Portobello FP	22	Grangemouth	4
Dundee HS FP	50	East Kilbride	7

DIVISION IV

Hutchesons'	6	Perthshire	36
Greenock Wands	6	St Boswells	16
Edinburgh Univ	31	Paisley	6
Peebles	45	Alloa	0
Leith Acads	32	Cambuslang	14
Cartha QP	8	Dumfries	12
Linlithgow	27	Penicuik	4

DIVISION V

Glenrothes	8	Livingston	10
Ardrossan Acads	9	Dunbar	6
Broughton FP	3	Hillfoots	11
Madras College FP	27	Murrayfield	9
Lismore	38	Aberdeen Univ	0
Moray	12	Lenzie	12

DIVISION VI

Carnoustie HS FP	12	Earlston	7
Stewartry	10	Drumpellier	3
Old Aloysians	25	Walkerburn	10
Panmure	12	St Andrews Univ	31
Harris Acad FP	20	Clydebank	9
North Berwick	9	Cumbernauld	4
Montrose	13	Marr	9

DIVISION VII

Dalkeith	6	Lasswade	20
Stobswell	7	Falkirk	26
Garioch	15	Ross High	14
Forrester FP	10	Rosyth & District	9
Cumnock	15	Birkmyre	6
Garnock	15	Strathmore	0
Irvine	3	Duns	20

November 18

DIVISION I

Stew/Melv FP	15	West of Scotland	7
Gala	7	Kelso	17
Jed-Forest	15	Edinburgh Acads	4
Selkirk	9	Heriot's FP	15
Melrose	8	Ayr	9
Stirling County	20	Boroughmuir	12
Hawick	25	Glasgow High/Kelv	10

DIVISION II

Langholm	0	Kilmarnock	12
Glasgow Acads	15	Preston Lodge FP	15
Corstorphine	37	Currie	34
Watsonians	19	Kirkcaldy	17
Dunfermline	7	Edinburgh Wands	24
Hillhead/Jord	17	Musselburgh	8
Dalziel HS FP	6	Gordonians	7

DIVISION III

Howe of Fife	21	Biggar	15
Morgan Acad FP	17	Trinity Acads	9
Highland	12	Haddington	7
Royal High	26	Aberdeen GS FP	4
Wigtownshire	13	Portobello FP	12
Grangemouth	6	Dundee HS FP	32
East Kilbride	3	Clarkston	3

DIVISION IV

Perthshire	16	Greenock Wands	0
St Boswells	43	Edinburgh Univ	0
Paisley	9	Peebles	22
Alloa	11	Leith Acads	25
Cambuslang	3	Cartha QP	18
Dumfries	0	Linlithgow	3
Penicuik	10	Hutchesons'	17

DIVISION V

Livingston	6	Ardrossan Acads	26
Dunbar	26	Broughton FP	3
Hillfoots	16	Waysiders	7
Aberdeenshire	16	Madras College FP	3
Murrayfield	6	Lismore	12
Aberdeen Univ	9	Moray	16
Lenzie	0	Glenrothes	16

DIVISION VI

Earlston	15	Stewartry	16
Drumpellier	7	Old Aloysians	3
Walkerburn	33	Panmure	15
St Andrews Univ	4	Harris Acad FP	0
Clydebank	10	North Berwick	13
Cumbernauld	35	Montrose	3
Marr	0	Carnoustie HS FP	23

DIVISION VII

Lasswade	21	Stobswell	9
Falkirk	25	Garioch	3
Ross High	9	Forrester FP	20
Rosyth & District	16	Cumnock	3
Birkmyre	0	Garnock	19
Strathmore	10	Irvine	9
Duns	25	Dalkeith	3

January 13

DIVISION I

Kelso	24	Stew/Melv FP	8
Edinburgh Acads	13	Gala	3
Heriot's FP	23	Jed-Forest	3
Ayr	15	Selkirk	25
Boroughmuir	10	Melrose	16
Glasgow High/Kelv	23	Stirling County	23
West of Scotland	3	Hawick	24

DIVISION II

Preston Lodge FP	37	Langholm	9
Currie	39	Glasgow Acads	17
Kirkcaldy	10	Corstorphine	12
Edinburgh Wands	30	Watsonians	17
Musselburgh	19	Dunfermline	6
Gordonians	7	Hillhead/Jord	12
Kilmarnock	31	Dalziel HS FP	30

DIVISION III

Trinity Acads	18	Howe of Fife	30
Haddington	24	Morgan Acad FP	7
Aberdeen GS FP	15	Highland	19
Portobello FP	6	Royal High	31
Dundee HS FP	25	Wigtownshire	16
Clarkston	25	Grangemouth	13
Biggar	7	East Kilbride	6

DIVISION IV

Edinburgh Univ	0	Perthshire	32
Peebles	13	St Boswells	15
Leith Acads	24	Paisley	8
Cartha QP	24	Alloa	9
Linlithgow	7	Cambuslang	6
Hutchesons'	23	Dumfries	4
Greenock Wands	7	Penicuik	13

DIVISION V

Broughton FP	6	Livingston	24
Waysiders	19	Dunbar	6
Madras College FP	6	Hillfoots	6
Lismore	32	Aberdeenshire	10
Moray	36	Murrayfield	7
Glenrothes	28	Aberdeen Univ	4
Ardrossan Acads	32	Lenzie	7

DIVISION VI

Old Aloysians	9	Earlston	9
Panmure	6	Drumpellier	22
Harris Acad FP	9	Walkerburn	0
North Berwick	24	St Andrews Univ	13
Montrose	19	Clydebank	12
Carnoustie HS FP	7	Cumbernauld	18
Stewartry	4	Marr	0

DIVISION VII

Garioch	0	Lasswade	7
Forrester FP	14	Falkirk	9
Cumnock	9	Ross High	8
Garnock	8	Rosyth & District	10
Irvine	44	Birkmyre	0
Dalkeith	7	Strathmore	9
Stobswell	16	Duns	7

January 27

DIVISION I

Stew/Melv FP	16	Gala	16
Jed-Forest	26	Selkirk	15
Melrose	32	Stirling County	6
Hawick	12	Kelso	10
West of Scotland	6	Edinburgh Acads	16
Ayr	12	Heriot's FP	16
Boroughmuir	11	Glasgow High/Kelv	13

DIVISION II

Langholm	23	Glasgow Acads	9
Corstorphine	26	Watsonians	10
Dunfermline	24	Hillhead/Jord	3
Dalziel HS FP	25	Preston Lodge FP	3
Kilmarnock	0	Currie	13
Edinburgh Wands	30	Kirkcaldy	9
Musselburgh	28	Gordonians	9

DIVISION III

Howe of Fife	16	Morgan Acad FP	7
Highland	13	Royal High	16
Wigtownshire	22	Grangemouth	9
Biggar	0	Haddington	7
Portobello FP	15	Aberdeen GS FP	4
Dundee HS FP	26	Clarkston	6

DIVISION IV

Perthshire	13	St Boswells	12
Paisley	31	Alloa	6
Greenock Wands	13	Peebles	26
Cartha QP	15	Leith Acads	16
Linlithgow	19	Hutchesons'	3

DIVISION V

Hillfoots	20	Aberdeenshire	0
Murrayfield	24	Aberdeen Univ	19
Lenzie	9	Broughton FP	6
Ardrossan Acads	15	Waysiders	0
Lismore	31	Madras College FP	3
Moray	3	Glenrothes	6

DIVISION VI

Earlston	28	Drumpellier	6
Walkerburn	9	St Andrews Univ	9
Clydebank	7	Cumbernauld	13
Marr	9	Old Aloysians	8
Stewartry	36	Panmure	10
North Berwick	23	Harris Acad FP	10
Montrose	40	Carnoustie HS FP	0

DIVISION VII

Ross High	15	Rosyth & District	9
Duns	14	Garioch	12
Irvine	21	Dalkeith	11

February 10

DIVISION I

Gala	10	Hawick	10
Selkirk	19	Stew/Melv FP	21
Stirling County	3	Jed-Forest	7
Melrose	22	Glasgow High/Kelv	10
Kelso	22	West of Scotland	10
Edinburgh Acads	22	Ayr	3
Heriot's FP	6	Boroughmuir	4

DIVISION II

Glasgow Acads	13	Dalziel HS FP	6
Watsonians	17	Langholm	6
Hillhead/Jord	10	Corstorphine	6
Dunfermline	30	Gordonians	0
Preston Lodge FP	12	Kilmarnock	9
Currie	21	Edinburgh Wands	9
Kirkcaldy	16	Musselburgh	21

DIVISION III

Morgan Acad FP	6	East Kilbride	6
Royal High	24	Howe of Fife	7
Grangemouth	0	Highland	15
Wigtownshire	13	Clarkston	21
Trinity Acads	24	Biggar	12
Haddington	20	Portobello FP	0
Aberdeen GS FP	4	Dundee HS FP	45

DIVISION IV

St Boswells	16	Penicuik	12
Alloa	6	Perthshire	18
Dumfries	27	Paisley	11
Cambuslang	19	Hutchesons'	15
Edinburgh Univ	19	Greenock Wands	13
Peebles	11	Cartha QP	6
Leith Acads	6	Linlithgow	4

DIVISION V

Dunbar	4	Lenzie	3
Aberdeenshire	16	Livingston	8
Aberdeen Univ	3	Hillfoots	15
Murrayfield	11	Glenrothes	4
Broughton FP	8	Ardrossan Acads	17
Waysiders	9	Lismore	0
Madras College FP	22	Moray	15

DIVISION VI

Drumpellier	3	Marr	12
St Andrews Univ	33	Earlston	3
Cumbernauld	18	Walkerburn	0
Clydebank	24	Carnoustie HS FP	9
Old Aloysians	10	Stewartry	22
Panmure	3	North Berwick	19
Harris Acad FP	19	Montrose	15

DIVISION VII

Falkirk	13	Duns	7
Rosyth & District	9	Lasswade	13
Strathmore	12	Ross High	13
Birkmyre	10	Dalkeith	6
Garioch	14	Stobswell	9
Forrester FP	22	Garnock	12
Cumnock	11	Irvine	7

February 24

DIVISION I

Hawick	9	Selkirk	12
Jed-Forest	20	Gala	18
Stirling County	15	West of Scotland	6
Glasgow High/Kelv	9	Heriot's FP	27
Ayr	11	Kelso	10
Boroughmuir	17	Edinburgh Acads	16

DIVISION II

Dalziel HS FP	33	Watsonians	18
Langholm	12	Dunfermline	20
Corstorphine	29	Glasgow Acads	0
Hillhead/Jord	7	Kilmarnock	32
Gordonians	0	Kirkcaldy	3
Edinburgh Wands	24	Preston Lodge FP	12
Musselburgh	9	Currie	14

DIVISION III

East Kilbride	12	Royal High	18
Howe of Fife	6	Wigtownshire	7
Highland	15	Morgan Acad FP	6
Portobello FP	12	Trinity Acads	12
Dundee HS FP	46	Haddington	7

DIVISION IV

Penicuik	10	Alloa	0
Perthshire	18	Cambuslang	3
Paisley	13	St Boswells	15
Dumfries	56	Greenock Wands	6
Hutchesons'	4	Leith Acads	6
Linlithgow	3	Peebles	27

DIVISION V

Lenzie	0	Aberdeenshire	0
Hillfoots	14	Dunbar	0
Aberdeen Univ	0	Ardrossan Acads	15
Glenrothes	25	Madras College FP	31
Lismore	16	Broughton FP	0
Moray	0	Waysiders	29

DIVISION VI

Marr	0	St Andrews Univ	16
Earlston	28	Clydebank	3
Walkerburn	13	Drumpellier	12
Cumbernauld	0	Stewartry	3
Carnoustie HS FP	13	Harris Acad FP	12
North Berwick	32	Old Aloysians	0
Montrose	9	Panmure	8

DIVISION VII

Duns	12	Rosyth & District	0
Lasswade	12	Birkmyre	0
Ross High	6	Falkirk	43
Strathmore	11	Stobswell	9
Dalkeith	10	Cumnock	0
Garnock	15	Garioch	12
Irvine	21	Forrester FP	3

March 10

DIVISION I

Selkirk	35	Stirling County	17
Stew/Melv FP	10	Hawick	26
Melrose	14	Jed-Forest	3
Gala	19	Heriot's FP	14
West of Scotland	37	Ayr	19
Kelso	20	Boroughmuir	26
Edinburgh Acads	17	Glasgow High/Kelv	10

DIVISION II

Watsonians	6	Hillhead/Jord	6
Langholm	16	Dalziel HS FP	19
Dunfermline	13	Corstorphine	9
Glasgow Acads	7	Kirkcaldy	21
Kilmarnock	3	Edinburgh Wands	19
Preston Lodge FP	9	Musselburgh	15
Currie	44	Gordonians	0

DIVISION III

Royal High	29	Grangemouth	4
Howe of Fife	28	East Kilbride	9
Wigtownshire	23	Highland	7
Morgan Acad FP	9	Aberdeen GS FP	18
Biggar	14	Portobello FP	12
Trinity Acads	12	Dundee HS FP	25
Haddington	15	Clarkston	18

DIVISION IV

Alloa	9	Dumfries	11
Perthshire	32	Penicuik	0
St Boswells	6	Leith Acads	17
Greenock Wands	7	Cartha QP	23
Edinburgh Univ	15	Linlithgow	0
Peebles	19	Hutchesons'	4

DIVISION V

Aberdeenshire	21	Aberdeen Univ	3
Livingston	9	Lenzie	11
Murrayfield	0	Hillfoots	21
Dunbar	4	Madras College FP	6
Ardrossan Acads	9	Lismore	10
Broughton FP	23	Moray	6
Waysiders	19	Glenrothes	3

DIVISION VI

St Andrews Univ	33	Cumbernauld	16
Earlston	12	Marr	15
Clydebank	4	Walkerburn	4
Stewartry	13	North Berwick	10
Panmure	15	Carnoustie HS FP	9

DIVISION VII

Rosyth & District	26	Strathmore	3
Lasswade	20	Duns	0
Falkirk	22	Cumnock	0
Stobswell	16	Garnock	22
Forrester FP	18	Dalkeith	0

National League Results
1973-1990

SCOTTISH CLUB CHAMPIONSHIP
1972-1973
(the last season of the old 'unofficial' Championship)

	P	W	L	D	F	A	Pts
Boro'muir F.P.	25	22	2	1	639	166	90
Hawick	27	22	3	2	765	213	85
Gala	27	23	4	0	837	268	85
Jordanhill	20	16	3	1	482	140	82
Langholm	22	17	3	2	516	202	81
Edin. Wanderers	22	16	6	0	443	249	72
Watsonians	22	16	6	0	484	278	72
Gordonians	15	10	5	0	342	165	66
W. of Scotland	19	12	6	1	371	220	65
Dunfermline	22	14	8	0	383	275	63
Glas. H.S.F.P.	25	15	9	1	589	355	62
Melrose	26	16	10	0	421	312	61
Ayr	20	12	8	0	358	258	60
Leith Acads	23	13	8	2	346	316	60
Hillhead F.P.	22	10	10	2	362	389	50
Glasgow Acads.	22	11	11	0	369	368	50
Selkirk	25	10	13	2	346	474	44
Kelso	27	12	15	0	389	538	44
Trinity Acads.	25	10	15	0	374	506	40
Edin. Acads	26	10	15	1	365	516	40
Jedforest	22	8	14	0	319	425	36
Hutchesons'	19	7	12	0	274	354	36
Broughton F.P.	15	5	10	0	149	267	33
Heriot's F.P.	24	7	16	1	446	481	31
Musselburgh	24	6	16	2	220	435	29
Perthshire	12	3	9	0	159	304	25
Royal H.S.F.P.	26	6	20	0	263	635	23
Aber. G.S.F.P.	19	4	15	0	194	419	21
Kelvin. Acads.	19	3	16	0	176	479	16
Edinburgh Univ	18	2	15	1	219	511	13
Stewart's F.P.	24	3	21	0	198	716	12
Glasgow Univ.	20	1	18	1	125	754	7

Only games between clubs in this table included

NATIONAL LEAGUE RESULTS 1973-74
DIVISION I

	P	W	L	D	F	A	Pts
Hawick	11	9	1	1	214	92	19
West of Scotland	11	9	1	1	178	73	19
Gala	10	6	4	0	175	94	12
Glasgow High	11	6	5	0	176	170	12
Edin. Wanderers	11	5	5	1	107	101	11
Melrose	11	5	5	1	120	146	11
Boroughmuir	11	5	6	0	142	114	10
Jordanhill	11	5	6	0	89	105	10
Watsonians	11	4	6	1	125	154	9
Heriot's F.P.	11	4	6	1	139	169	9
Langholm	11	3	6	2	137	192	8
Glasgow Acads.	10	0	10	0	52	244	0

DIVISION II

Kelso	11	10	1	0	244	59	20
Dunfermline	11	8	2	1	175	40	17
Stewart's/Melville	11	8	2	1	201	92	17
Selkirk	11	8	3	0	162	104	16
Jedforest	11	8	3	0	236	108	16
Hillhead	11	6	4	1	134	148	13
Edin. Academs.	11	4	6	1	95	143	9
Ayr	11	4	7	0	138	117	8
Hutchesons'	11	3	8	0	54	199	6
Royal High	11	3	8	0	110	239	6
Aberdeen G.S.F.P.	11	1	10	0	77	223	2
Edin. University	11	1	10	0	54	208	2

DIVISION III

Kilmarnock	10	9	0	1	226	61	19
Gordonians	10	8	2	0	225	56	16
Trinity Academs	10	6	3	1	189	66	13
Leith Academs.	10	6	3	1	123	93	13
Kelvinside Acads.	10	6	4	0	158	152	12
Broughton F.P.	10	5	4	1	133	76	11
Perthshire	10	5	5	0	136	110	10
Glasgow Univ.	10	3	7	0	67	176	6
Paisley G.S. F.P.	10	3	7	0	86	247	6
Allan Glen's F.P.	10	2	8	0	67	218	4
Musselburgh	10	0	10	0	50	205	0

DIVISION IV

	P	W	L	D	F	A	Pts
Highland	11	11	0	0	299	54	22
Haddington	11	10	1	0	241	71	20
Clarkston	11	8	3	0	233	80	16
Marr	11	7	4	0	181	136	14
Dundee H.S. F.P.	11	6	5	0	165	126	12
Howe of Fife	11	5	6	0	149	171	10
Kirkcaldy	11	5	6	0	103	158	10
Aberdeen Univ.	11	4	7	0	114	188	8
Panmure	11	3	8	0	87	191	6
Madras Coll F.P.	11	3	8	0	97	256	6
Ardrossan Acads	11	2	9	0	60	165	4
Greenock Wands.	11	2	9	0	91	224	4

DIVISION V (West)

Dalziel H.S. F.P.	13	13	0	0	354	43	26
Garnock	13	11	2	0	306	80	22
Old Aloysians	12	9	3	0	265	128	18
Hamilton Acads.	13	8	4	1	287	135	17
Dumfries	12	8	4	0	181	118	16
Lenzie	13	7	5	1	161	154	15
Cartha	12	7	5	0	234	144	14
Bellahouston A.	13	7	6	0	175	136	14
Wigtownshire	12	5	7	0	92	110	10
Cambuslang	13	4	9	0	118	300	8
Whitecraigs	13	2	9	2	77	169	6
Strathclyde Univ.	13	3	10	0	127	249	6
Craigielea	13	1	11	1	84	468	3
Queen's Park F.P.	13	1	11	1	47	277	3

DIVISION V (East)

Harris F.P.	8	8	0	0	184	44	16
Aberdeen W./A.	8	7	1	0	121	49	14
Dundee Univ.	8	6	2	0	131	55	12
R. (Dick) Vet. Col.	8	4	4	0	83	111	8
St Andrews Univ.	7	3	4	0	76	89	6
Morgan F.P.	8	3	5	0	84	77	6
Stirling County	8	2	5	1	66	131	5
Aberdeenshire	7	1	6	0	43	99	2
Alloa	8	0	7	1	39	172	1

S.R.U. CHAMPIONSHIP 1974-75
DIVISION I

	P	W	L	D	F	A	Pts
Hawick	11	10	1	0	273	77	20
Gala	11	9	2	0	184	102	18
Boroughmuir	11	8	3	0	140	130	16
Heriot's F.P.	11	5	5	1	143	124	11
Watsonians	11	5	5	1	134	136	11
Jordanhill	11	5	6	0	117	116	10
West of Scotland	11	4	6	1	122	119	9
Melrose	11	4	6	1	89	127	9
Kelso	11	4	6	1	121	168	9
Edin. Wanderers	11	4	6	1	117	185	9
Glasgow High	11	4	7	0	97	133	8
Dunfermline	11	1	10	0	72	212	2

DIVISION II

Langholm	11	9	1	1	259	97	19
Kilmarnock	11	8	1	2	203	33	18
Gordonians	11	9	2	0	253	98	18
Jedforest	11	7	3	1	208	102	15
Stewart's/Melville	11	7	4	0	136	143	14
Ayr	11	5	5	1	115	126	11
Royal High	11	5	6	0	119	145	10
Glasgow Acads.	11	4	6	1	146	227	9
Selkirk	11	4	7	0	101	157	8
Edin. Academs.	11	2	8	1	93	174	5
Hillhead	11	2	8	1	71	228	5
Hutchesons'	11	0	11	0	72	246	0

DIVISION III

Highland	11	10	1	0	284	51	20
Trinity Academs.	11	10	1	0	242	81	20
Leith Academs.	11	9	2	0	188	54	18
Haddington	11	8	3	0	265	94	16
Perthshire	11	8	3	0	182	68	16
Broughton F.P.	11	5	6	0	176	110	10
Aberdeen G.S. F.P.	11	4	7	0	124	128	8
Edin. University	11	4	7	0	72	171	8
Kelvinside Acads.	11	3	8	0	114	145	6
Glasgow Univ.	11	3	8	0	89	246	6
Allan Glen's F.P.	11	2	9	0	68	320	4
Paisley Gram.	11	0	11	0	29	365	0

DIVISION IV

	P	W	L	D	F	A	Pts
Marr	11	9	1	1	183	77	19
Harris Acad. F.P.	11	8	2	1	157	58	17
Howe of Fife	11	8	3	0	179	65	16
Kirkcaldy	11	7	3	1	166	115	15
Clarkston	11	6	3	2	175	67	14
Aberdeen Univ.	11	7	4	0	176	136	14
Dalziel H.S. F.P.	11	5	5	1	113	129	11
Dundee H.S. F.P.	10	4	6	0	158	118	8
Madras Coll. F.P.	10	3	7	0	96	156	6
Panmure	11	2	8	1	62	224	5
Musselburgh	11	2	9	0	76	149	4
Garnock	11	0	10	1	36	293	1

DIVISION V (East)

	P	W	L	D	F	A	Pts
Preston Lodge	13	12	1	0	426	73	24
Lasswade	13	11	1	1	243	98	23
Penicuik	12†	10	2	0	212	84	22
Dundee Univ.	13	8	5	0	222	144	16
Aberdeenshire	13	8	5	0	182	128	16
Morgan F.P.	13	7	5	1	173	151	15
Aberdeen W./A.	13	5	7	1	117	199	11
Corstorphine	13	5	8	0	126	139	10
Peebles	13	4	8	1	131	153	9
St Andrews Univ.	12†	4	7	1	156	179	9
Grangemouth	13	4	8	1	153	211	9
Alloa	13	4	8	1	101	173	9
Stirling County	12*	3	8	1	86	216	9
R. (Dick) Vet. Col.	12*	0	12	0	34	414	0

* Royal (Dick) Vet. College *v.* Stirling County 1/3/75 fixture not played but Stirling County awarded the 2 points.

† Penicuik *v.* St Andrews Univ. 9/11/74 fixture not played but Penicuik awarded the 2 points.

DIVISION V (West 'A')

	P	W	L	D	F	A	Pts
Ardrossan Acads	9	8	0	1	175	62	17
Greenock Wands.	9	8	1	0	215	54	16
Hamilton Acads.	9	7	2	0	130	77	14
Dumfries	9	6	3	0	119	119	12
Old Aloysians	9	4	3	2	91	107	10
Lenzie	9	4	5	0	101	98	8
Cartha Queen's Pk.	9	3	6	0	52	112	6
Bellahouston A.	8	1	7	0	68	145	2
Cambuslang	8	1	7	0	63	167	2
Wigtownshire	9	0	8	1	67	140	1

DIVISION V (West 'B')

	P	W	L	D	F	A	Pts
Hyndland	6	6	0	0	122	60	12
St Mungo's Acads.	6	4	1	1	73	27	9
Strathclyde Univ.	6	3	2	1	60	38	7
Whitecraigs	6	3	3	0	73	70	6
Uddingston	6	2	4	0	33	76	4
Craigielea	6	4	5	0	29	64	2
Lanark	6	1	5	0	24	99	2

S.R.U. CHAMPIONSHIP 1975-76

DIVISION I

Hawick	11	11	0	0	311	86	22
Gala	11	10	1	0	218	123	20
West of Scotland	11	7	3	1	183	96	15
Boroughmuir	11	6	5	0	140	111	12
Langholm	11	6	5	0	145	130	12
Jordanhill	11	5	5	1	185	140	11
Watsonians	11	5	6	0	137	146	10
Kilmarnock	11	4	6	1	115	162	9
Edin. Wanderers	11	4	7	0	121	200	8
Heriot's F.P.	11	3	8	0	113	289	6
Melrose	11	2	9	0	116	203	4
Kelso	11	1	9	1	105	203	3

DIVISION II

Highland	11	10	1	0	279	90	20
Selkirk	11	9	2	0	209	125	18
Stewart's/Melville	11	7	4	0	207	91	14
Gordonians	11	7	4	0	217	125	14
Jedforest	11	7	4	0	189	126	14
Glasgow High	11	5	5	1	173	164	11
Ayr	11	4	6	1	131	171	9
Edin. Acads.	11	4	6	1	114	187	9
Glasgow Acads.	11	4	7	0	137	147	8
Dunfermline	11	4	7	0	141	181	8
Royal High	11	2	7	2	74	216	6
Trinity Acads.	11	0	10	1	58	306	1

DIVISION III

	P	W	L	D	F	A	Pts
Haddington	11	10	1	0	246	50	20
Leith Acads.	11	10	1	0	274	80	20
Harris Acad. F.P.	11	6	3	2	219	36	14
Perthshire	11	6	4	1	148	142	13
Hillhead	11	6	5	0	195	120	12
Aberdeen G.S.F.P.	11	5	4	2	146	123	12
Edin. University	11	5	4	2	125	181	12
Hutchesons'	11	3	5	3	88	197	9
Marr	11	3	7	1	92	156	7
Broughton	11	3	8	0	108	213	6
Kelvinside Acads.	11	2	8	1	106	195	5
Glasgow Univ.	11	1	10	0	100	294	2

DIVISION IV

	P	W	L	D	F	A	Pts
Preston Lodge	11	9	2	0	239	68	18
Clarkston	11	8	2	1	229	75	17
Howe of Fife	11	8	3	0	180	106	16
Aberdeen Univ.	11	7	4	0	186	122	14
Ardrossan Acads.	11	6	3	2	182	123	14
Dalziel H.S.F.P.	11	5	4	2	115	121	12
Madras Coll. F.P.	11	4	6	1	115	120	9
Kirkcaldy	11	4	6	1	129	166	9
Allan Glen's F.P.	11	4	7	0	115	126	8
Dundee H.S. F.P.	11	3	6	2	81	141	8
Paisley Gram.	11	2	9	0	56	240	4
Panmure	11	1	9	1	37	256	3

DIVISION V

	P	W	L	D	F	A	Pts
Greenock Wans.	11	10	1	0	196	86	20
Dundee Univ.	11	10	1	0	182	86	20
Garnock	11	8	3	0	186	152	16
Penicuik	11	7	4	0	196	96	14
Morgan	11	7	4	0	126	93	14
Hamilton Acads.	11	5	6	0	146	150	10
Dumfries	11	5	6	0	119	167	10
Musselburgh	11	4	7	0	108	130	8
Old Aloysians	11	4	7	0	138	196	8
Lasswade	11	3	8	0	89	160	6
Lenzie	11	2	9	0	67	143	4
Aberdeenshire	11	1	10	0	92	186	2

DIVISION VI

	P	W	L	D	F	A	Pts
Cartha Q.P.	11	9	1	1	208	100	19
Cambuslang	11	7	3	1	149	100	15
Peebles	11	7	4	0	132	87	14
Bellahouston	11	7	4	0	162	118	14
Grangemouth	10*	6	4	0	128	100	14
Alloa	11	6	4	1	123	119	13
Hyndland	11	6	5	0	171	133	12
St. Andrews Univ.	10*	4	4	2	145	122	10
Corstorphine	10	4	6	0	106	94	8
St Mungo's	10	3	6	1	109	126	7
Aberdeen W./A.	11	1	10	0	86	211	2
Strathclyde Univ.	11	1	10	0	54	263	2

* St Andrews Univ. *v.* Grangemouth 4/10/75 fixture not played but Grangemouth awarded 2 points.

DIVISION VII

Dunbar	11	10	1	0	355	75	20
Moray	11	9	1	1	152	95	19
Drumpellier	11	9	2	0	292	52	18
Stirling County	11	8	3	0	197	69	16
Wigtownshire	11	4	5	2	172	95	10
Hillfoots	11	4	5	2	96	94	10
Whitecraigs	11	5	6	0	86	170	10
R. (Dick) Vet. Col.	11	4	6	1	96	198	9
Liberton	11	2	6	3	103	131	7
Lanark	11	2	6	3	107	180	7
Uddingston	11	2	9	0	50	295	4
Craigielea	11	1	10	0	41	293	2

S.R.U. CHAMPIONSHIP 1976-77

DIVISION I

Hawick*	11	9	2	0	301	115	18
Gala*	11	9	2	0	270	84	18
West of Scotland	11	9	2	0	190	80	18
Kilmarnock	11	7	4	0	197	171	14
Boroughmuir	11	6	4	1	156	121	13
Heriot's F.P.	11	5	4	2	172	143	12
Jordanhill	11	5	6	0	131	126	10
Highland	11	4	6	1	114	143	9
Watsonians	11	3	6	2	148	159	8
Langholm	11	3	8	0	65	232	6
Edin. Wanderers	11	3	8	0	112	282	6
Selkirk	11	0	11	0	93	293	0

* In a play-off at Melrose on 12.4.77 Hawick defeated Gala by 15-3.

DIVISION II

	P	W	L	D	F	A	Pts
Melrose	11	9	1	1	242	102	19
Stewart's/Melville	11	9	1	1	235	104	19
Gordonians	11	6	5	0	181	132	12
Kelso	11	5	4	2	166	150	12
Jedforest	11	5	6	0	142	113	10
Ayr	11	5	6	0	134	136	10
Edin. Acads.	11	4	5	2	96	144	10
Dunfermline	11	5	6	0	94	186	10
Haddington	11	3	5	3	124	123	9
Glasgow High	11	4	6	1	84	131	9
Leith Acads.	11	3	8	0	129	184	6
Glasgow Acads.	11	3	8	0	107	229	6

DIVISION III

Preston Lodge	11	10	1	0	212	80	20
Clarkston	11	9	1	1	219	55	19
Royal High	11	8	1	2	160	64	18
Edin. University	11	6	3	2	122	93	14
Trinity Acads.	11	5	4	2	129	109	12
Perthshire	11	5	4	2	110	127	12
Aberdeen G.S. F.P.	11	5	5	1	142	120	11
Harris Acad. F.P.	11	4	4	3	121	130	11
Hillhead	11	3	8	0	148	182	6
Marr	11	1	8	2	79	179	4
Broughton F.P.	11	1	9	1	52	218	3
Hutchesons'	11	1	10	0	69	206	2

DIVISION IV

Howe of Fife	11	10	1	0	185	77	20
Madras Coll. F.P.	11	7	4	0	180	77	14
Dalziel H.S. F.P.	11	7	4	0	132	123	14
Greenock Wands.	11	6	4	1	118	123	13
Allan Glen's F.P.	11	6	5	0	156	122	12
Aberdeen Univ.	10	6	4	0	140	112	12
Kelvinside Acads.	10	5	5	0	134	113	10
Ardrossan Acads.	11	5	6	0	159	137	10
Kirkcaldy	11	4	6	1	187	178	9
Dundee Univ.	11	4	7	0	104	122	8
Dundee H.S. F.P.	11	4	7	0	103	152	8
Glasgow Univ.	11	0	11	0	39	301	0

National League Results 1973-1990

DIVISION V

	P	W	L	D	F	A	Pts
Musselburgh	11	11	0	0	198	53	22
Penicuik	10	9	1	0	153	65	18
Cartha Q.P.	11	6	4	1	159	128	13
Dumfries	11	6	5	0	142	157	12
Hamilton Acads.	11	6	5	0	105	119	12
Lasswade	10	5	5	0	111	113	10
Morgan F.P.	10	5	5	0	112	146	10
Old Aloysians	11	4	6	1	167	170	9
Cambuslang	11	4	6	1	155	161	9
Garnock	10	3	6	1	126	145	7
Paisley Gram.	11	2	9	0	95	164	4
Panmure	11	1	10	0	82	184	2

DIVISION VI

	P	W	L	D	F	A	Pts
Corstorphine	11	10	0	1	191	63	21
Dunbar	11	9	2	0	239	66	18
Grangemouth	10	7	3	0	131	87	14
Bellahouston	11	5	5	1	152	108	11
Alloa	11	5	5	1	157	131	11
Peebles	11	5	6	0	128	133	10
St Andrews Univ	10	5	5	0	92	111	10
Aberdeenshire	10	5	5	0	122	142	10
St Mungo's Acads.	11	4	7	0	97	157	8
Moray	10	4	6	0	103	181	8
Hyndland	10	2	7	1	119	263	5
Lenzie	10	0	10	0	64	153	0

DIVISION VII

	P	W	L	D	F	A	Pts
Stirling County*	10	9	0	1	150	36	21
Dalkeith	11	10	1	0	274	91	20
Drumpellier	11	7	4	0	188	81	14
East Kilbride	11	6	4	1	166	144	13
Wigtownshire†	10	5	5	0	152	85	12
Hillfoots	11	6	5	0	174	115	12
R. (Dick) Vet. Coll.	11	5	6	0	134	154	10
Whitecraigs	11	5	6	0	106	136	10
Stobswell	10	4	6	0	151	155	8
Liberton F.P.	11	3	8	0	102	147	6
Aberdeen W./A.	10	2	8	0	67	156	4
Strathclyde Univ.	9	0	9	0	54	448	0

* Stirling County v. Strathclyde University 27.11.76 fixture not played but Stirling County awarded 2 points.

† Wigtownshire v. Strathclyde University 2.10.76 fixture not played but Wigtownshire awarded 2 points.

S.R.U. CHAMPIONSHIP 1977-78

DIVISION I

	P	W	L	D	F	A	Pts
Hawick	11	10	0	1	324	68	21
Boroughmuir	11	9	1	1	241	95	19
Kilmarnock	11	8	3	0	163	122	16
Heriot's F.P.	11	6	5	0	154	147	12
Langholm	10	5	5	0	118	181	10
West of Scotland	10	4	5	1	123	103	9
Jordanhill	11	3	6	2	104	140	8
Gala	10	4	6	0	139	177	8
Stewart's/Melville	10	4	6	0	127	178	8
Watsonians	11	3	7	1	74	162	7
Melrose	11	3	8	0	123	180	6
Highland	11	2	9	0	86	223	4

DIVISION II

Kelso	11	10	1	0	182	75	20
Haddington	11	8	3	0	149	101	16
Ayr	11	8	3	0	167	123	16
Jedforest	11	7	4	0	207	113	14
Gordonians	11	6	4	1	134	112	13
Selkirk	11	6	5	0	151	108	12
Edin. Acads.	11	4	6	1	122	132	9
Glasgow High	11	3	6	2	116	115	8
Clarkston	11	4	7	0	95	168	8
Edin. Wanderers	11	3	8	0	105	162	6
Dunfermline	11	3	8	0	108	254	6
Preston Lodge	11	2	9	0	121	194	4

DIVISION III

Leith Acads.	11	11	0	0	223	61	22
Madras Coll. F.P.	11	9	2	0	149	103	18
Royal High	11	8	3	0	212	78	16
Glasgow Acads.	11	8	3	0	217	111	16
Trinity Acads.	11	5	5	1	149	95	11
Howe of Fife	11	5	5	1	123	106	11
Harris Acad. F.P.	11	4	5	2	108	104	10
Hillhead	11	3	6	2	86	175	8
Perthshire	11	4	7	0	112	210	8
Edin. University	11	3	8	0	139	169	6
Aberdeen G.S. F.P.	11	3	8	0	89	165	6
Marr	11	0	11	0	54	284	0

National League Results 1973-1990

DIVISION IV

	P	W	L	D	F	A	Pts
Kelvinside Acads.........	11	9	2	0	162	92	18
Penicuik	11	8	2	1	199	65	17
Aberdeen Univ.	11	8	3	0	136	81	16
Musselburgh	11	5	4	2	110	94	12
Broughton F.P.	11	6	5	0	136	135	12
Kirkcaldy....................	11	6	5	0	108	157	12
Hutchesons'	11	5	6	0	87	117	10
Dundee Univ.	11	4	6	1	89	144	9
Dalziel H.S. F.P...........	11	4	7	0	120	107	8
Allan Glen's F.P.	11	3	7	1	92	109	7
Greenock Wands.	11	3	7	1	70	113	7
Ardrossan Acads.........	11	2	9	0	77	172	4

DIVISION V

Old Aloysians.............	11	9	2	0	184	97	18
Corstorphine..............	11	8	2	1	145	59	17
Dundee H.S. F.P.........	11	8	3	0	138	78	16
Hamilton Acads.........	11	7	3	1	111	108	15
Lasswade....................	11	7	4	0	91	100	14
Dumfries....................	11	5	5	1	130	119	11
Cambuslang	11	5	6	0	115	135	10
Garnock	11	4	6	1	120	130	9
Dunbar.......................	11	4	7	0	96	163	8
Morgan F.P.	11	3	8	0	112	96	6
Cartha Q.P..................	11	3	8	0	99	139	6
Glasgow Univ..............	11	1	10	0	86	203	2

DIVISION VI

Dalkeith......................	11	9	2	0	294	64	18
Stirling County	11	9	2	0	201	67	18
Peebles	11	9	2	0	221	93	18
Grangemouth	11	7	4	0	215	86	14
St Andrews Univ.........	11	6	5	0	217	99	12
Moray.........................	11	6	5	0	113	154	12
Bellahouston..............	11	5	6	0	121	212	10
Paisley Gram..............	11	4	7	0	107	157	8
St Mungo's Acads.	11	4	7	0	68	154	8
Alloa..........................	11	3	7	1	92	212	7
Aberdeenshire	11	2	8	1	116	189	5
Panmure	11	1	10	0	75	353	2

DIVISION VII

	P	W	L	D	F	A	Pts
Glenrothes	11	11	0	0	315	54	22
East Kilbride	11	10	1	0	307	67	20
Portobello	11	9	2	0	291	77	18
Stobswell	11	8	3	0	182	149	16
Drumpellier	10	6	4	0	140	132	12
Hyndland	11	4	6	1	99	219	9
Wigtownshire	11	4	6	1	94	164	9
Whitecraigs	11	3	7	1	81	136	7
R. (Dick) Vet. Coll.	11	3	8	0	100	304	6
Helensburgh	11	2	8	1	72	188	5
Hillfoots	11	2	9	0	86	206	4
Lenzie	10	1	9	0	78	149	2

S.R.U. CHAMPIONSHIP 1978-79

DIVISION I

Heriot's F.P.	11	10	1	0	246	82	20
Gala	11	8	3	0	150	106	16
Stewart's/Melville	10	7	3	0	144	78	14
Hawick	10	6	4	0	184	115	12
West of Scotland	10	5	4	1	116	92	11
Boroughmuir	11	5	5	1	120	106	11
Kelso	11	5	6	0	139	173	10
Kilmarnock	10	4	5	1	131	129	9
Watsonians	11	4	6	1	97	162	9
Jordanhill	11	3	8	0	133	153	6
Langholm	11	2	8	1	97	215	5
Haddington	11	2	8	1	79	225	5

DIVISION II

Melrose	11	10	0	1	228	78	21
Selkirk	11	10	1	0	270	103	20
Gordonians	9	5	3	1	183	68	11
Leith Academs.	10	5	4	1	109	115	11
Edin. Wanderers	11	4	5	2	115	112	10
Edin. Academs.	11	5	6	0	120	127	10
Jedforest	11	4	6	1	123	139	9
Ayr	11	4	6	1	124	163	9
Highland	10	4	6	0	92	130	8
Clarkston	11	3	7	1	97	237	7
Glasgow High	11	3	8	0	98	183	6
Madras Coll. F.P.	11	3	8	0	86	190	6

DIVISION III

	P	W	L	D	F	A	Pts
Royal High	11	10	1	0	215	95	20
Trinity Academs	11	8	3	0	174	88	16
Penicuik	11	7	2	2	111	92	16
Dunfermline	11	7	4	0	164	107	14
Harris Acad. F.P.	11	5	5	1	121	103	11
Howe of Fife	11	5	5	1	111	128	11
Hillhead	11	5	6	0	122	126	10
Glasgow Acads.	11	4	7	0	109	115	8
Kelvinside Acads.	11	4	7	0	108	129	8
Preston Lodge	11	4	7	0	104	129	8
Perthshire	11	3	6	2	79	163	8
Edin. University	11	1	10	0	56	199	2

DIVISION IV

Musselburgh	11	10	1	0	199	55	20
Kirkcaldy	11	9	2	0	183	75	18
Aberdeen Univ.	11	8	3	0	162	82	16
Dalziel H.S. F.P.	11	6	5	0	119	91	12
Corstorphine	10	6	4	0	117	90	12
Broughton F.P.	11	6	5	0	135	115	12
Allan Glen's F.P.	11	6	5	0	153	147	12
Aberdeen G.S. F.P.	10	5	5	0	145	131	10
Marr	11	4	7	0	99	121	8
Hutchesons'	11	3	8	0	107	145	6
Old Aloysians	10	1	9	0	84	263	2
Dundee Univ.	10	0	10	0	44	232	0

DIVISION V

Stirling County	11	10	0	1	217	57	21
Greenock Wands.	11	9	1	1	178	91	19
Ardrossan Acads.	11	5	4	2	156	93	12
Dalkeith	10	6	4	0	135	81	12
Dumfries	11	5	4	2	137	119	12
Cambuslang	10	6	4	0	83	96	12
Morgan A.F.P.	11	5	6	0	122	174	10
Hamilton Acads.	10	4	5	1	112	104	9
Dundee H.S. F.P.	10	4	6	0	88	135	8
Garnock	11	3	7	1	129	175	7
Dunbar	11	3	8	0	104	191	6
Lasswade	11	0	11	0	70	215	0

DIVISION VI

	P	W	L	D	F	A	Pts
Glenrothes	11	10	0	1	351	41	21
East Kilbride	10	8	1	1	175	25	17
Grangemouth	11	8	3	0	165	90	16
Paisley Gram.	11	7	4	0	133	104	14
Moray	10	5	5	0	101	114	10
St Andrews Univ.	10	5	5	0	143	163	10
Cartha Q.P.	11	4	6	1	107	149	9
Alloa	10	4	6	0	125	133	8
Peebles	9	3	5	1	79	82	7
Glasgow Univ.	11	3	8	0	36	184	6
St Mungo's Acads.	11	2	9	0	72	210	4
Bellahouston	11	2	9	0	69	261	4

DIVISION VII

	P	W	L	D	F	A	Pts
Portobello	11	11	0	0	317	73	22
Stewartry	11	8	2	1	123	65	17
Livingston	11	8	3	0	255	66	16
Strathmore	11	7	4	0	165	96	14
Drumpellier	11	7	4	0	138	92	14
Stobswell	11	4	5	2	204	112	10
Hyndland	11	4	6	1	106	132	9
Wigtownshire	11	4	7	0	88	181	8
Aberdeenshire	11	3	7	1	116	173	7
Whitecraigs	11	3	7	1	72	234	7
Panmure	11	3	8	0	118	166	6
R. (Dick) Vet. Coll.	11	1	10	0	37	349	2

S.R.U. CHAMPIONSHIP 1979-80

DIVISION I

	P	W	L	D	F	A	Pts
Gala	11	9	1	1	256	58	19
Heriot's F.P.	11	9	2	0	222	118	18
Hawick	10	7	3	0	223	101	14
Stewart's/Melville	11	6	5	0	140	137	12
Boroughmuir	11	5	5	1	136	171	11
Watsonians	10	3	4	3	92	148	9
Melrose	11	4	6	1	117	206	9
West of Scotland	11	4	7	0	142	149	8
Kelso	11	4	7	0	137	177	8
Kilmarnock	11	4	7	0	99	160	8
Selkirk	11	3	7	1	137	162	7
Jordanhill	11	3	7	1	72	186	7

DIVISION II

	P	W	L	D	F	A	Pts
Gordonians	11	9	2	0	180	87	18
Langholm	*10	8	2	0	180	99	18
Jedforest	11	7	4	0	166	122	14
Edinburgh Acads.	11	7	4	0	142	99	14
Highland	11	7	4	0	122	118	14
Royal High	11	5	5	1	114	138	11
Ayr	11	5	6	0	133	109	10
Clarkston	11	5	6	0	106	115	10
Leith Acads.	*10	4	5	1	74	127	9
Edin. Wanderers	11	3	8	0	89	121	6
Haddington	11	3	8	0	74	176	6
Trinity Acads.	11	1	10	0	76	145	2

* The Langholm *v.* Leith Academicals fixture on 26th January 1980 was not played and under Rule 9 Langholm was awarded the 2 Championship points.

DIVISION III

	P	W	L	D	F	A	Pts
Glasgow Acads.	11	10	1	0	259	81	20
Preston Lodge	11	10	1	0	133	78	20
Dunfermline	11	7	3	1	186	81	15
Howe of Fife	11	5	5	1	113	118	11
Hillhead	11	5	6	0	116	139	10
Musselburgh	11	5	6	0	69	119	10
Glasgow High	11	4	6	1	93	105	9
Madras Coll. F.P.	11	4	6	1	90	171	9
Harris Acad. F.P.	11	3	6	2	117	108	8
Kirkcaldy	11	3	6	2	92	122	8
Kelvinside Acads.	11	4	7	0	113	154	8
Penicuik	11	2	9	0	76	181	4

DIVISION IV

	P	W	L	D	F	A	Pts
Stirling County	10	9	0	1	172	40	19
Aberdeen G.S. F.P.	11	7	3	1	212	71	15
Corstorphine	11	6	5	0	96	128	12
Greenock Wands.	11	6	5	0	110	112	12
Broughton	11	5	6	0	151	111	10
Edinburgh Univ.	11	5	6	0	129	152	10
Allan Glen's	11	5	6	0	122	146	10
Aberdeen Univ.	10	4	5	1	135	155	9
Dalziel H.S. F.P.	11	4	6	1	84	141	9
Hutchesons'	11	4	6	1	90	162	9
Marr	11	4	7	0	95	164	8
Perthshire	11	3	7	1	121	135	7

DIVISION V

	P	W	L	D	F	A	Pts
Glenrothes	11	10	1	0	249	44	20
Cambuslang	11	9	2	0	116	98	18
Garnock	10	6	3	1	120	104	13
Dalkeith	10	5	4	1	119	94	11
Hamilton Acads.	11	5	5	1	119	149	11
Ardrossan Acads.	11	5	6	0	180	100	10
Dumfries	11	5	6	0	167	119	10
East Kilbride	9	5	4	0	119	116	10
Old Aloysians	11	5	6	0	109	181	10
Morgan F.P.	11	4	7	0	88	120	8
Dundee H.S. F.P.	11	3	7	1	101	157	7
Dundee Univ.	11	0	11	0	73	278	0

DIVISION VI

	P	W	L	D	F	A	Pts
Portobello F.P.	11	11	0	0	339	49	22
Grangemouth	11	9	2	0	249	81	18
Dunbar	11	7	4	0	128	89	14
Moray	11	7	4	0	174	147	14
Paisley Gram.	11	7	4	0	138	139	14
Cartha Q.P.	10	5	5	0	113	96	10
Stewartry	11	5	6	0	132	141	10
Alloa	11	5	6	0	113	129	10
Peebles	11	3	7	1	86	148	7
St Andrews Univ.	11	3	8	0	66	217	6
Glasgow Univ.	11	1	9	1	63	235	3
Lasswade	10	1	9	0	65	195	2

DIVISION VII

	P	W	L	D	F	A	Pts
Livingston	11	10	1	0	241	63	20
Drumpellier	11	9	1	1	226	63	19
Stobswell	10	7	3	0	207	66	14
Wigtownshire	11	7	4	0	112	115	14
Strathclyde Police	11	6	5	0	124	138	12
North Berwick	9	5	4	0	112	77	10
Strathmore	10	5	5	0	116	90	10
Aberdeenshire	11	4	6	1	89	126	9
Hillfoots	11	4	7	0	88	174	8
Hyndland F.P.	11	3	7	1	66	182	7
Bellahouston	11	1	9	1	66	195	3
St Mungo's Acads.	9	0	9	0	30	188	0

S.R.U. CHAMPIONSHIP 1980-81
DIVISION I

	P	W	L	D	F	A	Pts
Gala	11	11	0	0	237	55	22
Heriot's F.P.	11	10	1	0	269	103	20
Hawick	11	6	4	1	246	117	13
West of Scotland	11	6	4	1	167	116	13
Boroughmuir	11	6	4	1	131	142	13
Gordonians	11	5	5	1	156	165	11
Stewart's/Melville	11	4	5	2	121	122	10
Watsonians	11	5	6	0	79	148	10
Kelso	11	4	6	1	153	169	9
Melrose	11	3	7	1	93	155	7
Kilmarnock	11	1	8	2	77	190	4
Langholm	11	0	11	0	39	286	0

DIVISION II

	P	W	L	D	F	A	Pts
Selkirk	11	10	0	1	273	78	21
Jed-Forest	11	7	2	2	139	101	16
Preston Lodge	11	7	4	0	156	91	14
Jordanhill	11	6	3	2	144	88	14
Highland	11	5	4	2	89	114	12
Glasgow Acads.	11	5	5	1	117	165	11
Royal High	11	5	6	0	125	123	10
Clarkston	11	4	6	1	116	122	9
Leith Acads.	11	4	6	1	97	156	9
Edinburgh Acads.	11	3	6	2	98	106	8
Ayr	11	4	7	0	99	133	8
Edin. Wanderers	11	0	11	0	55	231	0

DIVISION III

	P	W	L	D	F	A	Pts
Haddington	11	9	2	0	189	111	18
Musselburgh	11	8	2	1	132	84	17
Dunfermline	11	6	3	2	150	106	14
Howe of Fife	11	7	4	0	127	84	14
Glasgow High	11	6	4	1	178	126	13
Trinity Acads.	11	6	5	0	155	153	12
Stirling County	11	4	5	2	144	160	10
Madras Coll. F.P.	11	4	6	1	94	82	9
Kirkcaldy	11	4	6	1	109	152	9
Hillhead	11	3	8	0	80	166	6
Harris Acad. F.P.	11	2	8	1	89	140	5
Aberdeen G.S. F.P.	11	2	8	1	114	197	5

DIVISION IV

	P	W	L	D	F	A	Pts
Dalziel H.S. F.P.	11	10	1	0	153	55	20
Aberdeen Univ.	11	9	2	0	170	102	18
Glenrothes	11	6	4	1	127	78	13
Penicuik	9	6	3	0	114	121	12
Hutchesons'	11	6	5	0	166	127	12
Corstorphine	10	5	5	0	152	99	10
Edinburgh Univ.	11	5	6	0	138	143	10
Broughton	11	5	6	0	140	163	10
Greenock Wands.	11	4	7	0	122	128	8
Allan Glen's	11	3	6	2	98	141	8
Cambuslang	11	3	7	1	98	143	7
Kelvinside Acads.	10	0	10	0	65	243	0

DIVISION V

	P	W	L	D	F	A	Pts
Portobello F.P.	10	10	0	0	206	73	20
Marr	11	8	3	0	127	77	16
East Kilbride	10	6	3	1	114	98	13
Perthshire	10	6	4	0	129	86	12
Grangemouth	11	6	5	0	142	106	12
Morgan F.P.	11	6	5	0	117	109	12
Dumfries	11	5	6	0	148	123	10
Garnock	11	5	6	0	109	163	10
Ardrossan Acads.	10	4	5	1	108	148	9
Old Aloysians	11	3	8	0	125	183	6
Dalkeith	11	2	9	0	73	151	4
Hamilton Acads.	11	2	9	0	65	146	4

DIVISION VI

	P	W	L	D	F	A	Pts
Livingston	11	9	2	0	172	73	18
Alloa	11	8	2	1	218	90	17
Dundee H.S. F.P.	11	8	2	1	166	52	17
Moray	11	7	4	0	122	99	14
Drumpellier	11	6	5	0	150	104	12
Cartha Q.P.	11	5	4	2	110	87	12
Stewartry	10	4	5	1	83	145	9
Dundee Univ.	10	4	6	0	96	102	8
Dunbar	11	4	7	0	83	169	8
Peebles	11	3	7	1	79	118	7
Paisley Gram.	11	1	7	3	64	107	5
St Andrews Univ.	11	1	9	1	60	257	3

DIVISION VII

	P	W	L	D	F	A	Pts
Currie	11	10	1	0	267	68	20
North Berwick	11	9	2	0	191	59	18
Wigtownshire	11	8	3	0	189	106	16
Stobswell	11	7	3	1	186	109	15
Panmure	11	7	4	0	206	125	14
Lenzie	11	5	5	1	157	106	11
Strathclyde Police	11	5	6	0	84	134	10
Hillfoots	11	4	7	0	118	157	8
Strathmore	11	4	7	0	93	151	8
Aberdeenshire	11	4	7	0	58	192	8
Glasgow Univ.	11	2	9	0	70	256	4
Lasswade	11	0	11	0	41	197	0

S.R.U. CHAMPIONSHIP

DIVISION I

Hawick	11	10	1	0	289	115	20
Heriot's F.P.	11	9	1	1	216	117	19
Gala	11	8	3	0	245	102	16
Kelso	11	8	3	0	203	130	16
Boroughmuir	11	6	5	0	154	154	12
Stewart's/Melville	11	5	6	0	210	192	10
Selkirk	11	4	6	1	154	189	9
West of Scotland	11	4	7	0	177	152	8
Watsonians	11	4	7	0	159	176	8
Jed-Forest	11	3	8	0	81	243	6
Melrose	11	2	9	0	96	235	4
Gordonians	11	2	9	0	94	273	4

DIVISION II

Kilmarnock	11	11	0	0	215	79	22
Royal High	11	8	3	0	180	102	16
Glasgow Acads.	11	8	3	0	143	134	16
Highland	10	6	3	1	158	78	13
Jordanhill	11	6	5	0	136	107	12
Edinburgh Acads.	10	5	5	0	109	124	10
Clarkston	11	5	6	0	117	132	10
Preston Lodge	11	4	6	1	119	120	9
Musselburgh	11	3	7	1	97	153	7
Leith Acads.	11	3	7	1	104	190	7
Langholm	11	3	8	0	97	112	6
Haddington	11	1	10	0	96	240	2

DIVISION III

	P	W	L	D	F	A	Pts
Ayr	11	9	0	2	171	63	20
Stirling County	11	8	2	1	184	92	17
Glasgow High	10	7	2	1	150	88	15
Howe of Fife	11	7	3	1	162	99	15
Trinity Acads.	10	5	4	1	123	111	11
Madras Coll. F.P.	11	5	5	1	105	120	11
Dunfermline	11	5	6	0	147	122	10
Aberdeen Univ.	11	4	6	1	95	120	9
Edin. Wanderers	11	4	7	0	130	133	8
Dalziel H.S. F.P.	11	3	8	0	81	171	6
Kirkcaldy	11	3	8	0	81	178	6
Hillhead	11	1	10	0	105	237	2

DIVISION IV

Broughton	11	9	1	1	162	74	19
Portobello F.P.	11	9	2	0	241	100	18
Harris Acad. F.P.	11	9	2	0	143	83	18
Hutchesons'	11	8	3	0	173	115	16
Aberdeen G.S. F.P.	11	7	3	1	170	102	15
Glenrothes	11	6	5	0	203	97	12
Greenock Wands.	11	5	5	1	206	111	11
Marr	11	4	6	1	99	123	9
Corstorphine	11	3	8	0	66	133	6
Allan Glen's	11	2	9	0	94	179	4
Edinburgh Univ.	11	2	9	0	106	227	4
Penicuik	11	0	11	0	40	359	0

DIVISION V

Morgan Acad. F.P.	11	9	1	1	200	93	19
Ardrossan Acads.	11	9	2	0	207	94	18
Dumfries	11	8	1	2	213	109	18
Perthshire	11	6	5	0	151	138	12
Garnock	11	6	5	0	109	123	12
Old Aloysians	10	5	4	1	152	156	11
Alloa	11	5	6	0	154	146	10
Cambuslang	11	4	5	2	149	147	10
Grangemouth	11	4	6	1	152	159	9
Livingston	11	3	7	1	89	147	7
Kelvinside Acads.	10	2	8	0	61	211	4
East Kilbride	11	0	11	0	68	182	0

DIVISION VI

	P	W	L	D	F	A	Pts
Dundee H.S. F.P.........	11	10	1	0	189	75	20
North Berwick	11	10	1	0	169	67	20
Currie...........................	11	9	2	0	222	66	18
Drumpellier	10	7	3	0	162	91	14
Cartha Q.P.	10	6	4	0	150	67	12
Moray..........................	10	4	6	0	95	129	8
Peebles	10	4	6	0	114	156	8
Hamilton Acads..........	11	4	7	0	108	157	8
Dunbar........................	11	3	8	0	81	172	6
Stewartry....................	11	2	8	1	79	160	5
Dundee Univ.	11	2	8	1	82	207	5
Dalkeith......................	11	2	9	0	84	188	4

DIVISION VII

Lenzie..........................	11	9	0	2	208	56	20
Stobswell	11	9	1	1	199	82	19
Walkerburn.................	11	8	3	0	186	92	16
Crieff..........................	11	7	3	1	168	139	15
Panmure	11	7	4	0	246	106	14
Cumbernauld..............	11	6	4	1	154	95	13
Wigtownshire.............	11	5	6	0	152	111	10
Paisley Gram.	11	4	6	1	112	144	9
Hillfoots	11	3	7	1	108	167	7
Strathclyde Police	11	3	7	1	92	207	7
Strathmore.................	11	1	10	0	69	229	2
St Andrews Univ.........	11	0	11	0	50	316	0

S.R.U. CHAMPIONSHIP 1982-83

DIVISION I

Gala............................	13	12	1	0	491	116	24
Hawick	12	11	1	0	355	88	22
Heriot's F.P.	13	10	3	0	259	150	20
Kelso	13	9	4	0	261	138	18
Boroughmuir..............	13	9	4	0	210	106	18
Stewart's/Melville	12	7	5	0	223	159	14
Selkirk........................	12	7	5	0	178	156	14
Watsonians.................	12	7	5	0	189	169	14
West of Scotland.........	12	5	7	0	193	203	10
Melrose	13	3	8	2	136	201	8
Kilmarnock	13	3	10	0	114	337	6
Jed-Forest	12	2	9	1	113	211	5
Royal High..................	13	1	11	1	86	339	3
Gordonians	13	0	13	0	57	492	0

DIVISION II

	P	W	L	D	F	A	Pts
Ayr	13	10	2	1	207	100	21
Haddington	13	9	2	2	239	117	20
Langholm	13	10	3	0	199	136	20
Edinburgh Acads.	13	9	3	1	271	142	19
Preston Lodge	13	9	3	1	210	129	19
Stirling County	12	8	4	0	156	126	16
Glasgow Acads.	12	7	4	1	222	144	15
Glas High/K'side	13	5	8	0	171	192	10
Highland	13	5	8	0	154	190	10
Howe of Fife	13	3	9	1	89	176	7
Clarkston	13	3	9	1	117	211	7
Jordanhill	13	3	10	0	124	209	6
Musselburgh	13	3	10	0	107	249	6
Leith Acads.	13	2	11	0	91	236	4

DIVISION III

	P	W	L	D	F	A	Pts
Aberdeen G.S. F.P.	13	10	1	2	216	119	22
Portobello F.P.	13	10	2	1	197	82	21
Edin. Wanderers	13	9	4	0	223	111	18
Hutchesons'	13	8	4	1	187	122	17
Madras Coll. F.P.	13	8	5	0	189	121	16
Hillhead	13	5	6	2	130	119	12
Glenrothes	13	5	6	2	135	152	12
Trinity Acads.	13	5	7	1	145	103	11
Dunfermline	13	4	6	3	140	156	11
Kirkcaldy	13	5	7	1	98	133	11
Dalziel H.S. F.P.	13	4	6	3	81	160	11
Aberdeen Univ.	12	5	7	0	93	161	10
Harris Acad. F.P.	13	4	9	0	73	143	8
Broughton	12	0	12	0	88	313	0

DIVISION IV

	P	W	L	D	F	A	Pts
Greenock Wands.	13	12	1	0	266	102	24
Cambuslang	13	11	2	0	204	95	22
Alloa	13	9	4	0	186	135	18
Allan Glen's	13	8	4	1	161	122	17
Morgan Acad. F.P.	12	8	4	0	242	120	16
Marr	13	8	5	0	141	141	16
Perthshire	13	6	7	0	111	178	12
Dumfries	13	5	7	1	194	156	11
Ardrossan Acads.	13	5	7	1	134	166	11
Edinburgh Univ.	12	5	7	0	135	167	10
Old Aloysians'	13	4	8	1	126	170	9
Corstorphine	12	3	8	1	130	171	7
Garnock	13	1	11	1	90	205	3
Penicuik	12	1	11	0	78	270	2

DIVISION V

	P	W	L	D	F	A	Pts
Grangemouth	13	12	1	0	268	66	24
Currie	13	10	3	0	252	82	20
Cartha Q.P.	13	9	3	1	258	110	19
Dundee H.S. F.P.	12	8	4	0	197	82	16
Livingston	13	8	5	0	173	164	16
North Berwick	13	7	6	0	129	135	14
Drumpellier	12	6	5	1	105	120	13
Peebles	12	6	6	0	98	134	12
Stewartry	12	5	7	0	91	199	10
East Kilbride	12	4	8	0	98	145	8
Moray	12	4	8	0	125	187	8
Hamilton Acads.	13	3	10	0	89	173	6
Dundee Univ.	13	3	10	0	104	262	6
Dunbar	13	2	11	0	84	212	4

DIVISION VI

	P	W	L	D	F	A	Pts
Lenzie	13	12	1	0	331	121	24
Lismore	13	10	3	0	262	87	20
Cumbernauld	13	9	3	1	181	112	19
Stobswell	13	9	4	0	252	130	18
Hillfoots	13	8	5	0	194	130	16
Walkerburn	12	7	4	1	183	97	15
Wigtownshire	13	7	6	0	146	125	14
Dalkeith	12	6	6	0	153	151	12
Crieff	12	5	7	0	156	139	10
Panmure	12	4	7	1	264	165	9
Strathclyde Police	13	3	8	2	132	181	8
Paisley	13	4	9	0	165	237	8
Strathmore	12	1	11	0	62	349	2
St Andrews Univ.	12	0	11	1	78	535	1

DIVISION VII

	P	W	L	D	F	A	Pts
Linlithgow	13	10	2	1	202	66	21
Uddingston	12	9	3	0	235	128	18
Biggar	13	7	4	2	167	101	16
Montrose	13	8	5	0	154	109	16
Earlston	13	7	5	1	150	131	15
Falkirk	13	7	6	0	165	146	14
Hyndland	12	7	5	0	135	119	14
Stirling Univ.	12	6	5	1	156	122	13
Cumnock	12	6	5	1	160	135	13
Waid Academy F.P.	13	5	5	3	125	149	13
Strathendrick	13	5	7	1	135	193	11
Lanark	13	4	9	0	151	220	8
Carrick	13	3	10	0	87	185	6
Irvine	13	0	13	0	73	291	0

S.R.U. CHAMPIONSHIP 1983-84

DIVISION I

	P	W	L	D	F	A	Pts
Hawick	13	13	0	0	477	53	26
Gala	13	12	1	0	299	75	24
Stewart's/Melville	13	9	4	0	327	151	18
Kelso	13	9	4	0	266	161	18
Heriot's F.P.	12	8	3	1	258	145	17
Watsonians	13	8	5	0	203	190	16
Boroughmuir	12	7	5	0	215	205	14
Selkirk	13	5	8	0	215	222	10
West of Scotland	13	4	9	0	194	303	8
Jed-Forest	13	3	9	1	142	216	7
Melrose	13	3	9	1	118	243	7
Ayr	12	3	8	1	87	310	7
Kilmarnock	13	2	9	2	155	286	6
Haddington	12	0	12	0	64	460	0

DIVISION II

Glasgow Acads.	12	10	1	1	268	114	21
Edinburgh Acads.	13	10	3	0	172	102	20
Portobello F.P.	13	9	4	0	198	121	18
Stirling County	13	8	5	0	210	155	16
Preston Lodge	13	6	6	1	165	143	13
Gordonians	13	6	6	1	162	174	13
Langholm	12	6	5	1	110	182	13
Highland	13	6	7	0	160	164	12
Clarkston	13	5	7	1	194	193	11
Jordanhill	13	5	7	1	128	168	11
Royal High	13	5	8	0	147	207	10
Howe of Fife	13	4	8	1	133	159	9
Glas High/K'side	13	3	9	1	140	209	7
Aberdeen G.S. F.P.	13	3	10	0	107	194	6

DIVISION III

Edin. Wanderers	13	12	1	0	245	91	24
Dunfermline	13	10	2	1	240	64	21
Musselburgh	13	10	2	1	182	95	21
Cambuslang	13	7	6	0	131	162	14
Dalziel H.S. F.P.	13	6	7	0	119	138	12
Greenock Wand.	13	6	7	0	112	196	12
Hutchesons'	13	5	7	1	115	132	11
Hillhead	13	5	7	1	156	178	11
Leith Acads.	13	5	7	1	101	131	11
Kirkcaldy	13	5	8	0	105	127	10
Madras F.P.	13	5	8	0	87	122	10
Trinity Acads.	13	5	8	0	140	178	10
Aberdeen Univ.	13	4	8	1	163	200	9
Glenrothes	13	3	10	0	135	217	6

National League Results 1973-1990

DIVISION IV

	P	W	L	D	F	A	Pts
Perthshire	13	11	2	0	205	92	22
Morgan F.P.	13	10	3	0	263	104	20
Alloa	13	10	3	0	199	119	20
Corstorphine	13	8	3	2	164	115	18
Grangemouth	13	6	6	1	151	114	13
Dumfries	13	6	6	1	147	123	13
Harris F.P.	12	5	5	2	135	123	12
Broughton	13	6	7	0	131	185	12
Marr	13	4	6	3	127	144	11
Currie	13	5	6	0	156	139	10
Edinburgh Univ.	12	5	7	0	141	137	10
Allan Glen's	13	4	8	1	101	212	9
Ardrossan Acads.	13	3	10	0	104	275	6
Old Aloysians'	13	1	12	0	73	215	2

DIVISION V

	P	W	L	D	F	A	Pts
Dundee H.S. F.P.	13	12	0	1	329	40	25
Lenzie	13	11	2	0	211	131	22
Peebles	13	9	3	1	183	114	19
Stewartry	13	7	6	0	146	162	14
Penicuik	13	7	6	0	145	189	14
Cartha Q.P.	13	6	6	1	157	152	13
Drumpellier	13	6	6	1	123	158	13
Livingston	13	6	7	0	125	145	12
Lismore	13	6	7	0	145	175	12
East Kilbride	13	5	7	1	143	196	11
Moray	13	4	8	1	130	151	9
Hamilton Acads.	13	4	9	0	106	177	8
Garnock	13	2	9	2	132	191	6
North Berwick	13	1	10	2	82	176	4

DIVISION VI

	P	W	L	D	F	A	Pts
Panmure	13	11	1	1	242	89	23
Hillfoots	13	11	2	0	253	134	22
Linlithgow	12	8	2	2	277	86	18
Crieff	12	8	4	0	210	104	16
Dalkeith	13	7	5	1	198	193	15
Strathclyde Police	13	6	7	0	129	178	12
Dunbar	12	5	7	0	107	124	10
Cumbernauld	12	5	7	0	119	147	10
Stobswell	13	5	8	0	171	210	10
Dundee Univ.	11	5	6	0	111	202	10
Walkerburn	13	5	8	0	114	217	10
Paisley	13	4	8	1	143	226	9
Wigtownshire	13	4	9	0	120	157	8
Uddingston	13	1	11	1	108	235	3

DIVISION VII

	P	W	L	D	F	A	Pts
Earlston	13	12	1	0	210	66	24
Biggar	13	11	1	1	276	68	23
Waysiders	13	9	3	1	223	142	19
Montrose	12	8	4	0	174	110	16
Edin. Northern	13	7	5	1	142	160	15
Waid Academy F.P.	13	5	5	3	144	104	13
Hyndland	13	5	5	3	105	106	13
Aberdeenshire	13	5	7	1	207	128	11
Falkirk	13	5	7	1	150	202	11
Stirling Univ.	13	5	8	0	125	248	10
Strathmore	13	4	8	1	116	186	9
Cumnock	13	4	9	0	123	174	8
St Andrews Univ.	13	3	9	1	113	262	7
Strathendrick	12	0	11	1	75	227	1

S.R.U. CHAMPIONSHIP 1984-85

DIVISION I

	P	W	L	D	F	A	Pts
Hawick	13	12	1	0	412	132	24
Kelso	13	10	2	0	374	96	20
Heriot's F.P.	12	9	3	0	217	140	18
Boroughmuir	12	8	4	0	214	150	16
Stewart's/Melville	13	7	6	0	220	176	14
Gala	12	7	0	5	226	213	14
Edinburgh Acads.	13	7	6	0	147	183	14
Melrose	13	5	7	1	162	204	11
Selkirk	12	5	6	1	125	188	11
Jedforest	13	4	8	1	150	204	9
Watsonians	12	4	8	0	138	241	8
West of Scotland	13	3	10	0	139	232	6
Ayr	13	3	10	0	102	225	6
Glasgow Acads.	13	2	10	1	149	391	5

DIVISION II

	P	W	L	D	F	A	Pts
Kilmarnock	13	10	2	1	193	95	21
Preston Lodge FP	13	9	2	2	213	110	20
*Dunfermline	13	8	4	1	184	128	17
Edin. Wanderers	12	8	4	0	193	121	16
Langholm	11	7	3	1	171	125	15
Haddington	13	7	6	0	164	142	14
Stirling County	13	6	6	1	197	159	13
*Howe of Fife	13	6	6	1	140	128	13
Royal High	13	5	5	3	102	118	13
Portobello	10	5	5	0	122	139	10
Jordanhill	13	5	8	0	128	177	10
Clarkston	13	5	8	0	126	188	10
Gordonians	12	1	11	0	140	251	2
Highland	12	1	11	0	66	259	2

* Awarded 2 Championship points against Portobello F.P. who were unable to fulfil the fixtures due to disciplinary action taken against them.

DIVISION III

	P	W	L	D	F	A	Pts
Musselburgh	13	10	1	2	239	89	22
*Glas. High/K'side	13	11	2	0	215	75	22
*Dalziel H.S. F.P.	12	8	4	0	118	110	16
Greenock Wand.	13	6	5	2	162	154	14
Aberdeen G.S. F.P.	12	6	5	1	109	97	13
Perthshire	13	6	6	1	148	165	13
Kirkcaldy	13	5	5	3	134	169	13
Hillhead	13	6	7	0	142	146	12
Cambuslang	11	5	5	1	144	132	11
Hutchesons'	13	5	7	1	170	195	11
Morgan Acad. F.P.	13	5	8	0	169	184	10
Madras F.P.	13	4	7	2	138	176	10
Leith Acads.	13	4	7	2	87	144	10
Trinity Acads.	13	1	11	1	71	210	3

* Awarded 2 Championship points against Cambuslang who were unable to fulfil the fixtures due to disciplinary action taken against them.

DIVISION IV

	P	W	L	D	F	A	Pts
Corstorphine	13	12	1	0	240	87	24
Edinburgh Univ.	13	12	1	0	249	113	24
Grangemouth	13	11	2	0	188	103	22
Currie	13	7	5	1	188	194	15
Dundee H.S. F.P.	13	7	6	0	191	165	14
Alloa	12	6	6	0	185	118	12
Dumfries	12	6	6	0	136	141	12
Lenzie	11	5	6	0	148	128	10
Broughton F.P.	12	5	7	0	89	185	10
Harris Acad. F.P.	12	3	6	3	131	179	9
Marr	13	4	9	0	111	214	8
Glenrothes	13	3	9	1	148	176	7
Allan Glen's	13	3	9	1	112	157	7
Aberdeen Univ.	11	0	11	0	54	210	0

DIVISION V

	P	W	L	D	F	A	Pts
Cartha Q.P.	13	12	1	0	275	64	24
Peebles	13	11	2	0	298	93	22
Hillfoots	13	8	4	1	154	111	17
Moray	12	7	4	1	135	104	15
Panmure	12	7	5	0	166	110	14
East Kilbride	12	7	5	0	136	143	14
Ardrossan Acads.	13	4	5	4	137	122	12
Lismore	13	6	7	0	151	184	12
Penicuik	13	5	8	0	134	216	10
Livingston	12	4	7	1	115	178	9
Hamilton Acads.	12	4	8	0	121	174	8
Drumpellier	13	3	8	2	107	193	8
Stewartry	13	3	9	1	108	206	7
Old Aloysians	12	2	10	0	53	192	4

DIVISION VI

	P	W	L	D	F	A	Pts
Biggar	13	11	2	0	194	107	22
Linlithgow	13	10	2	1	171	96	21
Earlston	12	7	4	1	159	94	15
Strathclyde Police	13	7	5	1	143	129	15
North Berwick	12	7	4	1	133	127	15
Dunbar	11	6	4	1	120	119	13
Stobswell	11	5	5	1	110	92	11
Cumbernauld	13	5	7	1	145	143	11
Paisley	12	5	7	0	155	138	10
Walkerburn	12	5	7	0	129	130	10
Dalkeith	13	5	8	0	153	168	10
Crieff	13	5	8	0	112	170	10
Dundee Univ.	12	3	8	1	106	174	7
Garnock	12	1	11	0	81	224	2

DIVISION VII

Wigtownshire	13	11	2	0	236	69	22
Montrose	13	11	2	0	210	110	22
Aberdeenshire	13	10	2	1	216	64	21
Waysiders	13	9	2	2	252	79	20
Murrayfield	13	9	4	0	334	101	18
Clydebank	13	8	5	0	188	131	16
Waid Acad. F.P.	13	6	7	0	134	158	12
Uddingston	12	5	6	1	101	165	11
Edin. Northern	13	5	8	0	142	176	10
Falkirk	12	4	8	0	132	155	8
Stirling Univ.	12	4	8	0	87	250	8
Rosyth & Dist.	12	2	10	0	52	250	4
Hyndland	13	2	11	0	44	256	4
Strathmore	13	1	12	0	66	230	2

SCHWEPPES NATIONAL LEAGUE 1985-86
DIVISION I

Hawick	13	12	1	0	241	117	24
Kelso	12	10	2	0	266	94	20
Stewart's-Melville F.P.	12	9	3	0	289	103	18
Watsonians	13	8	5	0	214	145	16
Heriot's F.P.	13	8	5	0	201	161	16
Gala	12	7	5	0	202	153	14
West of Scotland	12	7	5	0	199	192	14
Boroughmuir	13	7	6	0	143	163	14
Jedforest	13	5	8	0	132	218	10
Melrose	13	4	9	0	149	170	8
Edinburgh Acads	13	4	9	0	115	206	8
Selkirk	13	4	9	0	118	208	8
Preston Lodge	13	3	10	0	90	258	6
Kilmarnock	13	1	12	0	123	294	2

National League Results 1973-1990

DIVISION II

	P	W	L	D	F	A	Pts
Glasgow Acads............	12	12	0	0	214	93	24
Ayr...............................	13	9	4	0	308	118	18
Stirling County	13	9	4	0	178	110	18
Musselburgh	12	8	4	0	154	104	16
Glasgow High/K'side ..	12	7	5	0	158	185	14
Dunfermline	12	6	6	0	148	149	12
Haddington	12	6	6	0	153	160	12
Royal High.................	13	6	7	0	124	158	12
Howe of Fife..............	13	5	7	1	201	146	11
Langholm....................	13	5	7	1	133	134	11
Edin. Wanderers.........	12	5	6	1	128	181	11
Portobello F.P.	12	5	7	0	120	136	10
Clarkston....................	12	1	10	1	72	216	3
Jordanhill...................	11	0	11	0	42	243	0

DIVISION III

Corstorphine...............	12	12	0	0	273	49	24
Hillhead	13	10	3	0	186	142	20
Highland.....................	13	7	5	1	218	130	15
Perthshire	12	7	5	0	129	118	14
Hutchesons'	13	6	7	0	158	148	12
Gordonians	13	6	7	0	107	111	12
Cambuslang	12	6	6	0	131	150	12
Greenock Wands	12	6	6	0	137	171	12
Kirkcaldy....................	13	5	7	1	136	166	11
Aberdeen G.S. F.P......	13	5	8	0	126	174	10
Morgan F.P.	13	5	8	0	151	208	10
Dalziel H.S. F.P..........	13	4	8	1	138	136	9
Madras F.P..................	13	4	8	1	132	200	9
Edinburgh U...............	13	4	9	0	105	224	8

DIVISION IV

Currie..........................	13	12	1	0	269	65	24
Dundee H.S. F.P.........	13	12	1	0	245	93	24
Cartha Queen's Park ..	13	11	2	0	235	94	22
Peebles	12	9	3	0	155	94	18
Grangemouth	13	8	5	0	172	155	16
Dumfries.....................	12	6	6	0	97	186	12
Harris F.P.	11	5	6	0	101	129	10
Alloa...........................	12	5	7	0	90	131	10
Trinity Acads..............	13	4	9	0	107	141	8
Broughton	13	4	9	0	116	202	8
Glenrothes	11	3	7	1	75	119	7
Leith Acads.................	12	3	9	0	132	142	6
Lenzie.........................	13	2	10	1	114	186	5
Marr............................	13	2	11	0	83	254	4

DIVISION V

	P	W	L	D	F	A	Pts
East Kilbride	13	12	1	0	301	74	24
Biggar	13	11	2	0	200	101	22
Ardrossan Acads	12	9	3	0	197	120	18
Hillfoots	12	8	3	1	217	86	17
Moray	11	7	4	0	189	121	14
Lismore	12	7	5	0	171	148	14
Linlithgow	12	5	6	1	130	88	11
Livingston	11	5	6	0	82	171	10
Aberdeen University	12	4	7	1	172	141	9
Drumpellier	13	4	9	0	112	186	8
Penicuik	13	4	9	0	117	259	8
Panmure	11	3	7	1	119	260	7
Hamilton Acads	12	2	10	0	90	183	4
Allan Glen's F.P.	13	2	11	0	75	234	4

DIVISION VI

Wigtownshire	12	11	0	1	312	62	23
Crieff	13	9	3	1	167	142	19
Dunbar	12	8	4	0	206	91	16
Earlston	13	6	4	3	123	100	15
North Berwick	13	6	5	2	118	134	14
Paisley	13	6	6	1	156	100	13
Montrose	12	5	6	1	127	141	11
Stathclyde Police	13	5	7	1	97	138	11
Old Aloysians	11	4	5	2	98	138	10
Dalkeith	13	4	7	2	114	179	10
Walkerburn	12	5	7	0	81	180	10
Stewartry	13	4	8	1	114	126	9
Cumbernauld	13	4	8	1	78	142	9
Stobswell	13	3	10	0	114	232	6

DIVISION VII

St Boswells	12	11	1	0	235	76	22
Murrayfield	13	10	3	0	267	109	20
Aberdeenshire	13	10	3	0	257	116	20
Clydebank	12	8	3	1	142	93	17
Dundee University	11	7	4	0	178	135	14
Garioch	11	6	4	1	166	95	13
Waid F.P.	12	6	6	0	181	146	12
Falkirk	12	6	6	0	127	132	12
Cumnock	12	5	7	0	213	126	10
Waysiders	12	5	7	0	215	138	10
Edinburgh Northern	13	5	8	0	109	212	10
Garnock	11	2	9	0	74	139	4
Uddingston	12	2	10	0	64	295	4
Stirling University	12	0	12	0	29	445	0

McEWAN'S NATIONAL LEAGUE 1986-87

DIVISION I

	P	W	L	D	F	A	Pts
Hawick	13	12	1	0	366	148	24
Kelso	13	12	1	0	297	129	24
Watsonians	13	8	4	1	261	151	17
Stewart's Melville F.P.	13	7	6	0	210	184	14
Selkirk	13	7	6	0	215	236	14
West of Scotland	13	6	6	1	204	205	13
Boroughmuir	13	6	7	0	205	189	12
Melrose	13	5	6	2	166	185	12
Glasgow Acads	13	5	8	0	159	272	10
Heriot's F.P.	13	4	8	1	189	199	9
Edinburgh Acads	12	4	7	1	137	204	9
Ayr	13	4	8	1	122	227	9
Gala	13	4	9	0	150	264	8
Jed-Forest	12	2	9	1	109	197	5

DIVISION II

Kilmarnock	13	12	1	0	341	103	24
Musselburgh	13	10	3	0	229	112	20
Glasgow High/K'side	13	7	5	1	186	137	15
Stirling County	13	7	5	1	155	123	15
Hillhead	13	6	5	2	147	159	14
Preston Lodge F.P.	13	6	6	1	157	153	13
Royal High	13	6	6	1	126	153	13
Edin. Wanderers	13	6	7	0	166	162	12
Dunfermline	13	4	6	3	138	157	11
Howe of Fife	13	5	7	1	116	164	11
Portobello F.P.	13	5	8	0	93	183	10
Corstorphine	13	4	8	1	179	174	9
Haddington	13	4	8	1	106	197	9
Langholm	13	3	10	0	86	248	6

DIVISION III

Currie	13	12	1	0	329	93	24
Jordanhill	13	9	3	1	182	123	19
Morgan Acad. F.P.	12	7	4	1	155	111	15
Perthshire	13	7	6	0	194	169	14
Dundee H.S. F.P.	13	7	6	0	168	148	14
Dalziel H.S. F.P.	13	6	6	1	137	129	13
Kirkcaldy	13	6	6	1	131	158	13
Aberdeen G.S. F.P.	13	6	7	0	175	211	12
Gordonians	13	5	7	1	175	165	11
Greenock Wands.	12	5	6	1	95	142	11
Clarkston	12	4	7	2	145	185	10
Highland	13	5	8	0	140	209	10
Hutchesons'	13	4	9	0	127	206	8
Cambuslang	13	3	10	0	91	195	6

DIVISION IV

	P	W	L	D	F	A	Pts
East Kilbride	13	11	2	0	247	118	22
Cartha Queen's Park	13	11	2	0	225	129	22
Trinity Academicals	13	10	3	0	243	116	20
Leith Academicals	13	9	3	1	192	81	19
Alloa	13	6	6	1	146	131	13
Peebles	13	6	6	1	144	156	13
Biggar	13	6	6	1	155	169	13
Dumfries	13	6	6	1	129	147	13
Grangemouth	13	5	7	1	114	123	11
Edinburgh University	12	5	7	0	136	196	10
Broughton	13	5	8	0	115	186	10
Glenrothes	13	4	8	1	107	191	9
Harris Academy F.P.	12	2	9	1	107	204	5
Madras College F.P.	13	0	13	0	95	208	0

DIVISION V

	P	W	L	D	F	A	Pts
Wigtownshire	13	11	0	2	250	40	24
Lenzie	12	10	1	1	225	68	21
Linlithgow	13	9	2	2	156	61	20
Hillfoots	13	7	5	1	170	141	15
Ardrossan Acads	13	7	5	1	147	146	15
Lismore	12	7	5	0	249	134	14
Livingston	13	6	7	0	119	152	12
Marr	13	5	7	1	168	160	11
Penicuik	12	5	7	0	140	164	10
Aberdeen University	11	5	6	0	112	172	10
Moray	13	5	8	0	118	198	10
Panmure	13	4	8	1	144	175	9
Crieff	13	1	11	1	95	334	3
Drumpellier	12	1	11	0	80	228	2

DIVISION VI

	P	W	L	D	F	A	Pts
St Boswells	13	13	0	0	245	53	26
Paisley	13	10	2	1	263	83	21
North Berwick	13	10	2	1	145	96	21
Murrayfield	13	8	5	0	232	147	16
Stewartry	13	8	5	0	158	161	16
Montrose	13	7	6	0	118	148	14
Earlston	13	7	6	0	104	135	14
Dunbar	13	4	6	3	215	141	11
Walkerburn	13	4	7	2	108	159	10
Dalkeith	12	4	7	1	124	155	9
Old Aloysians	13	4	8	1	113	157	9
Strathclyde Police	12	3	7	2	93	126	8
Hamilton Acads	13	2	10	1	74	207	5
Allan Glen's	13	0	13	0	36	260	0

DIVISION VII

	P	W	L	D	F	A	Pts
Waysiders	13	12	0	1	223	69	25
Aberdeenshire	13	11	2	0	211	91	22
Stobswell F.P.	13	10	3	0	193	140	20
Clydebank	13	9	4	0	184	114	18
Falkirk	13	8	5	0	173	169	16
Carnoustie H.S. F.P.	13	6	5	2	221	140	14
Cumnock	13	6	7	0	178	192	12
Cumbernauld	13	6	7	0	114	146	12
Duns	13	5	8	0	109	119	10
Dundee University	13	4	8	1	187	220	9
Garioch	13	3	8	2	87	152	8
Edinburgh Northern	13	3	9	1	128	176	7
Waid Academy F.P.	13	2	10	1	91	255	5
Birkmyre	13	2	11	0	103	219	4

District League Champions (promoted to national league) East – Lasswade   West – Garnock   Midlands – St Andrews University

McEWAN'S NATIONAL LEAGUE 1987-88

DIVISION I

Kelso	13	12	1	0	343	108	24
Hawick	13	12	1	0	317	113	24
Melrose	13	10	3	0	273	140	20
Boroughmuir	13	7	4	2	206	152	16
Heriot's F.P.	13	6	7	0	188	220	12
Watsonians	13	6	7	0	137	239	12
Ayr	13	5	7	1	178	178	11
West of Scotland	13	5	7	1	189	214	11
Stew/Melv. F.P.	13	5	7	1	203	249	11
Glasgow Acads.	13	5	7	1	156	219	11
Selkirk	13	5	8	0	161	190	10
Edinburgh Acads.	13	4	8	1	136	208	9
Musselburgh	13	3	9	1	124	250	7
Kilmarnock	13	2	11	0	139	270	4

DIVISION II

Jed Forest	13	11	2	0	338	85	22
Glasgow High/Kelv.	13	11	2	0	353	104	22
Gala	13	11	2	0	306	109	22
Stirling County	13	11	2	0	327	141	22
Currie	13	11	2	0	239	113	22
Corstorphine	13	6	7	0	221	226	12
Preston Lodge F.P.	13	6	7	0	137	149	12
Edinburgh Wands	13	5	8	0	183	221	10
Dunfermline	13	5	8	0	149	209	10
Portobello F.P.	13	5	8	0	123	212	10
Howe of Fife	13	4	9	0	106	192	8
Hillhead	13	3	10	0	146	310	6
Royal High	13	2	11	0	114	297	4
Jordanhill	13	0	13	0	59	433	0

DIVISION III

	P	W	L	D	F	A	Pts
Langholm	13	10	2	1	218	112	21
Dalziel H.S. F.P.	13	10	3	0	192	109	20
Dundee H.S. F.P.	13	9	3	1	206	123	19
Kirkcaldy	13	8	5	0	139	94	16
East Kilbride	12	8	4	0	159	135	16
Highland	13	6	5	2	196	132	14
Greenock Wands	12	6	5	1	102	126	13
Morgan Acad F.P.	13	6	6	1	121	176	13
Clarkston	13	6	7	0	131	166	12
Gordonians	11	4	6	1	123	134	9
Aberdeen G.S. F.P.	13	4	9	0	142	158	8
Haddington	13	3	8	2	131	172	8
Perthshire	13	3	9	1	121	196	7
Cartha Q.P.	13	1	12	0	101	249	2

DIVISION IV

	P	W	L	D	F	A	Pts
Trinity Acads	13	11	2	0	231	100	22
Biggar	13	10	3	0	179	99	20
Grangemouth	13	8	3	2	238	171	18
Leith Acads	12	8	3	1	145	114	17
Edinburgh Univ.	13	8	5	0	201	147	16
Hutchesons'	13	7	5	1	178	142	15
Cambuslang	13	7	6	0	184	158	14
Dumfries	13	6	6	1	135	145	13
Peebles	13	6	7	0	142	135	12
Wigtownshire	13	5	7	1	157	185	11
Lenzie	13	5	8	0	147	218	10
Alloa	13	3	9	1	112	206	7
Broughton F.P.	13	2	11	0	111	215	4
Glenrothes	12	0	11	1	91	216	1

DIVISION V

	P	W	L	D	F	A	Pts
Linlithgow	13	11	1	1	259	28	23
St Boswells	12	10	2	0	184	127	20
Paisley	13	9	3	1	174	87	19
Lismore	13	7	5	1	138	144	15
Hillfoots	13	6	6	1	104	127	13
Aberdeen Univ.	11	6	5	0	149	98	12
Livingston	12	6	6	0	129	111	12
Madras College F.P.	13	6	7	0	133	140	12
Marr	13	5	7	1	120	137	11
Ardrossan Acads	12	5	7	0	110	106	10
Penicuik	12	5	7	0	106	174	10
Moray	13	3	8	2	76	165	8
Panmure	13	4	9	0	110	232	8
Harris Acad F.P.	13	1	11	1	84	200	3

DIVISION VI

	P	W	L	D	F	A	Pts
Murrayfield	13	12	1	0	223	36	24
Dunbar	13	11	1	1	263	77	23
Waysiders	13	10	2	1	279	72	21
Montrose	13	8	5	0	273	122	16
North Berwick	13	7	6	0	232	154	14
Aberdeenshire	12	7	5	0	160	111	14
Walkerburn	13	7	6	0	178	178	14
Earlston	13	6	7	0	128	134	12
Stewartry	13	4	8	1	139	120	9
Dumpellier	13	4	8	1	92	165	9
Old Aloysians	13	4	9	0	167	181	8
Dalkeith	13	4	9	0	97	259	8
Strathclyde Police	13	4	9	0	48	232	8
Crieff	12	0	12	0	53	491	0

DIVISION VII

	P	W	L	D	F	A	Pts
Carnoustie H.S. F.P.	13	12	1	0	370	82	24
St. Andrews Univ.	13	11	1	1	297	111	23
Falkirk	13	10	2	1	193	62	21
Clydebank	12	8	4	0	163	155	16
Duns	13	7	5	1	161	97	15
Cumnock	13	6	6	1	230	166	13
Lasswade	13	6	6	1	122	99	13
Garnock	12	6	6	0	112	128	12
Cumbernauld	12	5	7	0	137	145	10
Stobswell	12	5	7	0	109	178	10
Garioch	12	4	7	1	95	153	9
Allan Glen's	13	2	10	1	70	280	5
Hamilton Acads.	12	1	10	1	67	252	3
Dundee Univ.	13	1	12	0	134	352	2

District League Champions (promoted to national league). Edinburgh — Forrester F.P. Glasgow — Birkmyre Midlands — Rosyth & District.

McEWAN'S NATIONAL LEAGUE 1988-89

DIVISION I

	P	W	L	D	F	A	Pts
Kelso	13	10	3	0	357	111	20
Boroughmuir	13	9	2	2	314	145	20
Hawick	13	10	3	0	280	161	20
Edinburgh Acads.	13	8	3	2	242	127	18
Heriot's F.P.	13	9	4	0	301	196	18
Jed-Forest	13	8	4	1	270	164	17
Selkirk	13	7	5	1	175	153	15
West of Scotland	13	5	7	1	164	263	11
Stewart's Melville F.P.	13	5	7	1	168	278	11
Melrose	12	5	7	0	208	162	10
Ayr	13	4	8	1	202	271	9
Glasgow High/K'side	13	3	9	1	144	258	7
Glasgow Acads.	12	2	10	0	112	225	4
Watsonians	13	0	13	0	97	520	0

DIVISION II

	P	W	L	D	F	A	Pts
Stirling County	13	13	0	0	391	103	26
Gala	13	11	2	0	376	107	22
Currie	13	9	4	0	277	151	18
Kilmarnock	13	8	5	0	172	186	16
Edinburgh Wands.	13	7	5	1	231	172	15
Preston Lodge F.P.	13	7	6	0	184	139	14
Musselburgh	13	5	6	2	175	234	12
Hillhead/Jordanhill	13	5	7	1	152	237	11
Corstorphine	13	4	7	2	165	225	10
Dalziel H.S. F.P.	12	5	7	0	163	257	10
Langholm	12	3	6	3	132	238	9
Dunfermline	13	4	9	0	144	250	8
Portobello F.P.	13	3	9	1	136	247	7
Howe of Fife	13	1	12	0	144	296	2

DIVISION III

Kirkcaldy	12	12	0	0	263	77	24
Gordonians	11	8	2	1	188	115	17
Trinity Acads.	12	8	4	0	233	138	16
Dundee H.S. F.P.	11	7	4	0	173	121	14
Biggar	12	5	5	2	116	144	12
Haddington	11	6	5	0	159	188	12
Royal High	11	5	6	0	153	140	10
East Kilbride	11	5	6	0	119	140	10
Highland	12	4	7	1	159	185	9
Morgan Acads F.P.	12	4	8	0	136	186	8
Aberdeen G.S. F.P.	12	4	8	0	132	185	8
Clarkston	11	4	7	0	126	188	8
Greenock Wands.	12	1	11	0	85	235	2

DIVISION IV

Wigtownshire	13	11	1	1	253	71	23
Grangemouth	13	11	1	1	207	89	23
Peebles	13	11	1	1	192	77	23
Linlithgow	13	8	5	0	205	113	16
Leith Acads.	13	6	5	2	180	135	14
Edinburgh Univ.	13	7	6	0	173	198	14
Cambuslang	12	6	6	0	164	154	12
Perthshire	13	5	6	2	162	209	12
Hutchesons'	13	5	8	0	123	212	10
Dumfries	13	4	8	1	135	154	9
Cartha Queen's Park	13	4	8	1	97	126	9
St Boswells	13	3	10	0	97	168	6
Alloa	13	3	10	0	102	283	6
Lenzie	12	1	10	1	93	194	3

DIVISION V

	P	W	L	D	F	A	Pts
Paisley	13	12	1	0	292	92	24
Penicuik	13	12	1	0	209	79	24
Madras Coll. F.P.	13	9	4	0	177	109	18
Ardrossan Acads	12	8	3	1	164	107	17
Hillfoots	13	7	5	1	150	188	15
Dunbar	13	6	7	0	185	137	12
Livingston	13	6	7	0	134	172	12
Murrayfield	13	5	7	1	146	166	11
Lismore	12	3	5	4	126	165	10
Glenrothes	13	4	8	1	142	147	9
Aberdeen Univ.	13	3	8	2	136	176	8
Broughton F.P.	13	3	8	2	140	190	8
Moray	13	3	8	2	107	172	8
Marr	13	1	10	2	59	267	4

DIVISION VI

Aberdeenshire	13	10	1	2	255	55	22
Waysiders	12	9	2	1	222	62	19
Carnoustie H.S. F.P.	13	8	5	0	223	81	16
St. Andrews Univ.	12	8	4	0	172	97	16
Harris Acad. F.P.	13	5	5	3	145	138	13
Montrose	13	5	6	2	150	146	12
Earlston	13	6	7	0	146	181	12
Panmure	13	5	6	2	125	229	12
Old Aloysians	13	5	7	1	93	229	11
Stewartry	13	4	7	2	133	152	10
Drumpellier	13	4	7	2	105	173	10
Walkerburn	13	5	8	0	108	199	10
North Berwick	13	4	8	1	164	164	9
Dalkeith	13	4	9	0	102	237	8

DIVISION VII

Clydebank	11	11	0	0	205	63	22
Cumbernauld	12	9	2	1	209	84	19
Falkirk	12	9	3	0	202	107	18
Duns	12	7	5	0	160	120	14
Cumnock	11	7	4	0	172	149	14
Lasswade	11	6	5	0	159	82	12
Stobswell	12	6	6	0	91	148	12
Forrester F.P.	12	5	7	0	133	165	10
Garioch	12	5	7	0	125	184	10
Rosyth & District	12	4	7	1	119	149	9
Garnock	12	3	8	1	90	146	7
Birkmyre	11	1	9	1	78	182	3
Strathclyde Police	12	0	10	2	78	242	2

District League Champions (promoted to national league)
West – Irvine   Midland – Strathmore   East – Ross High.

McEWAN'S NATIONAL LEAGUE 1989-90

DIVISION I

	P	W	L	D	F	A	Pts
Melrose	12	10	1	1	247	107	21
Heriot's F.P.	13	10	3	0	276	132	20
Jed-Forest	13	10	3	0	203	149	20
Edinburgh Acads.	13	9	4	0	212	145	18
Stirling County	13	7	5	1	207	216	15
Boroughmuir	13	7	6	0	240	150	14
Glasgow H/K'side	13	6	6	1	181	195	13
Gala	13	5	6	2	187	223	12
Hawick	13	5	7	1	187	173	11
Selkirk	13	5	8	0	235	268	10
Kelso	13	4	8	1	195	221	9
Stew/Melville F.P.	12	4	7	1	140	225	9
Ayr	13	3	10	0	139	281	6
West of Scotland	13	1	12	0	126	308	2

DIVISION II

Edinburgh Wands.	13	12	1	0	332	147	24
Currie	13	10	2	1	299	177	21
Kilmarnock	13	7	4	2	213	168	16
Preston Lodge F.P.	13	7	5	1	209	177	15
Hillhead/Jordanhill	13	7	5	1	140	213	15
Musselburgh	13	6	5	2	189	162	14
Corstorphine	13	6	6	1	226	194	13
Glasgow Acads.	13	5	7	1	225	230	11
Watsonians	13	4	7	2	187	218	10
Langholm	13	5	8	0	192	226	10
Dunfermline	13	5	8	0	161	219	10
Kirkcaldy	13	4	8	1	163	181	9
Dalziel H.S. F.P.	13	4	9	0	203	266	8
Gordonians	13	3	10	0	114	294	6

DIVISION III

Dundee H.S. F.P.	13	12	0	1	446	100	25
Royal High	13	10	2	1	286	130	21
Wigtownshire	13	10	3	0	217	159	20
Clarkston	12	8	3	1	157	178	17
Portobello F.P.	13	6	6	1	155	168	13
Biggar	12	6	6	0	127	156	12
Howe of Fife	13	5	8	0	215	186	10
Grangemouth	12	5	7	0	151	195	10
Highland	13	5	8	0	114	212	10
Aberdeen G.S. F.P.	12	5	7	0	125	235	10
Trinity Acads.	13	4	8	1	182	220	9
Haddington	13	4	9	0	148	200	8
East Kilbride	13	3	8	2	147	202	8
Morgan Acad. F.P.	13	2	10	1	113	244	5

National League Results 1973-1990

DIVISION IV

	P	W	L	D	F	A	Pts
Perthshire	13	11	2	0	289	90	22
Peebles	13	10	3	0	311	99	20
Cartha Q.P.	13	9	4	0	175	131	18
Leith Acads.	13	9	4	0	181	176	18
St Boswells	13	8	5	0	204	143	16
Dumfries	12	8	4	0	202	152	16
Linlithgow	13	7	6	0	128	135	14
Hutchesons'	13	5	7	1	189	189	11
Cambuslang	11	5	6	0	97	147	10
Penicuik	12	5	7	0	133	226	10
Edinburgh Univ.	12	4	8	0	91	187	8
Greenock Wands.	13	3	9	1	129	220	7
Paisley	12	2	10	0	135	223	4
Alloa	13	1	12	0	96	241	2

DIVISION V

	P	W	L	D	F	A	Pts
Lismore	13	11	2	0	262	83	22
Waysiders	13	11	2	0	230	101	22
Hillfoots	13	10	2	1	213	65	21
Ardrossan Acads.	13	10	3	0	191	83	20
Madras Coll. F.P.	13	9	3	1	194	171	19
Aberdeenshire	13	6	6	1	134	176	13
Dunbar	12	6	6	0	170	95	12
Murrayfield	12	6	6	0	139	167	12
Glenrothes	13	4	9	0	119	140	8
Livingston	11	4	7	0	116	164	8
Moray	13	3	9	1	135	231	7
Broughton F.P.	13	3	10	0	109	201	6
Lenzie	13	2	9	2	80	193	6
Aberdeen Univ.	13	1	12	0	99	319	2

DIVISION VI

	P	W	L	D	F	A	Pts
North Berwick	13	12	1	0	205	85	24
Stewartry	13	11	1	1	192	134	23
St. Andrews Univ.	13	10	2	1	307	120	21
Cumbernauld	13	10	3	0	234	110	20
Harris Acads. F.P.	12	6	6	0	132	157	12
Earlston	13	5	7	1	195	162	11
Clydebank	13	5	7	1	176	148	11
Montrose	12	5	6	1	138	168	11
Drumpellier	12	5	7	0	100	141	10
Carnoustie H.S. F.P.	13	5	8	0	164	208	10
Marr	13	5	8	0	105	150	10
Walkerburn	13	3	8	2	131	196	8
Panmure	13	2	11	0	123	273	4
Old Aloysians	12	1	10	1	103	263	3

DIVISION VII

	P	W	L	D	F	A	Pts
Lasswade	13	11	1	1	200	83	23
Falkirk	13	11	2	0	378	75	22
Forrester F.P.	13	11	2	0	237	108	22
Duns	13	9	4	0	189	114	18
Rosyth & District	13	9	4	0	186	121	18
Irvine	12	6	6	0	222	120	12
Garioch	12	6	6	0	136	158	12
Cumnock	13	6	7	0	143	165	12
Garnock	13	6	7	0	151	185	12
Ross High	13	5	7	1	185	192	11
Birkmyre	13	3	10	0	110	269	6
Strathmore	13	3	10	0	88	271	6
Stobswell	13	2	11	0	113	305	4
Dalkeith	13	1	12	0	84	248	2

District League Champions (promoted to national league)
Edinburgh – Holy Cross   Glasgow – Whitecraigs Midlands – RAF Kinloss.

International Results

Season 1989-90

International matches – Scotland

25.10.89	Scotland – 38	Fiji – 17
9.12.89	Scotland – 32	Romania – 0
6.1.90	International Trial Match	Blues – 45 Reds – 4
3.2.90	Ireland – 10	Scotland – 13
17.2.90	Scotland – 21	France – 0
3.3.90	Wales – 9	Scotland – 13
17.3.90	Scotland – 13	England – 7

Scotland 'B' International matches

9.12.89 Scotland 'B' – 22   Ireland 'B' – 22
21.1.90 France 'B' – 31   Scotland 'B' – 9

Scotland Under-21 International match

28.4.90 Scotland U-21 – 10   Wales U-21 – 24

Other U-21 Representative matches

14.3.90 Scottish U-21 – 21   Combined Services U-21 – 4
28.4.90 Scottish U-21 – 8   Scottish Students – 19

Scottish U-18 Representative match

24.3.90 Scottish U-18 – 27   Scottish Schools – 7

Scotland U-18 Representative match

Netherlands U-18 – 0   Scotland – 32

Scotland U-19 Representative match

28.4.90 Scotland U-19 – 9   England U-19 – 17

Scottish Schools International matches

6.1.90 Wales – 15   Scotland – 0
31.3.90 Scotland – 19   Japan – 31
2.4.90 Scotland – 6   England – 32
14.4.90 Ireland – 14   Scotland – 10

Under-15 match

2.4.90 Scotland U-15 – 0   Wales U-15 – 22

Other International matches

4.11.89	England – 58 Fiji – 23
	Wales – 9 New Zealand – 34
18.11.89	Ireland – 6 New Zealand – 23
20.1.90	Wales – 19 France – 29
	England – 23 Ireland – 0
3.2.90	France – 7 England – 26
17.2.90	England – 34 Wales – 6
3.3.90	France – 31 Ireland – 12
24.3.90	Ireland – 14 Wales – 8

Other Representative matches

2.9.89	Connacht – 6 Glasgow – 21
4.9.89	Munster – 18 Glasgow – 18
4.10.89	Roxburghshire U-18 – 51 Selkirkshire – 3
21.10.89	Anglo Scots – 10 London Scottish – 21
1.11.89	South Dist. Union – 27 Glasgow Dist. Union – 0
	Edinburgh Dist. Union – 40 Midlands Dist. Union – 18
15.11.89	Glasgow U-18 – 51 North & Midlands U-18 – 3
	Edinburgh U-18 – 22 Edinburgh Schools – 6
	Glasgow Dist. Union – 13 Midlands Dist. Union – 26
	Edinburgh Dist. Union – 6 South Dist. Union – 22
21.11.89	Midlands U-21 – 15 North U-18 – 18
22.11.89	Edinburgh U-18 – 18 South U-18 – 20
2.12.89	North & Midlands U-18 – 19 Edinburgh U-18 – 19
	South U-18 – 24 Glasgow U-18 – 6
	Anglo Scots U-21 – 21 South U-21 – 21
16.12.89	North & Midlands U-18 – 0 South U-18 – 15
	Edinburgh U-18 – 10 Glasgow U-18 – 18
	Anglo Scots U-21 – 6 Edinburgh U-21 – 21
31.1.90	Edinburgh U-21 – 17 North & Midlands U-21 – 15
14.2.90	North & Midlands U-21 – 3 South U-21 – 52
28.2.90	North & Midlands U-21 – 16 Glasgow U-21 – 21
7.4.90	District Select U-18/U-19 XV – 28 Japan – 23

Scottish Students International matches

27.11.89	Oxford University – 28 Scottish Students – 25
6.12.89	Scottish Universities – 28 Scottish Combined Colleges – 3
16.2.90	Scottish Students – 6 French Students – 12
16.3.90	Scottish Universities – 8 English Universities – 30

Scotland Tour to New Zealand, May-June 1990

Gisbourne, 30.5.90
East Coast/Poverty Bay – 0   Scotland – 45

Wellington, 2.6.90
Wellington – 16   Scotland – 16

Nelson, 6.6.90
Nelson Bays/Marlborough – 6   Scotland – 23

Christchurch 9.6.90
Canterbury – 12   Scotland – 21

International Results

Invercargill, 12.6.90
Southland – 12   Scotland – 45

Palmerston North, 19.6.90
Manawatu – 4   Scotland – 19

Test Matches

Dunedin, 16.6.90
New Zealand – 31   Scotland – 16

Auckland, 23.6.90
New Zealand – 21   Scotland – 18